Heavy Weather Tactics Using Sea Anchors & Drogues

BY EARL R. HINZ

Sail Before Sunset, 1979

Understanding Sea Anchors & Drogues, 1987

Pacific Wanderer, 1991

Pacific Island Battlegrounds of World War II: Then and Now, 1995

The Offshore Log, Sixth Edition, 1997

Landfalls of Paradise: The Cruising Guide to the Pacific Islands, Fourth Edition, 1999

The Complete Book of Anchoring and Mooring, Second Edition, 1999

Heavy Weather Tactics Using Sea Anchors & Drogues, 2000

Heavy Weather Tactics Using Sea Anchors & Drogues

BY EARL R. HINZ

With drawings by RICHARD R. RHODES

Paradise Cay Publications
Arcata, California 95518
U.S.A.

Printed in the United States of America
First Edition

ISBN 0-939837-37-4

Published by
Paradise Cay Publications
P.O. Box 29
Arcata, California, 95521
800-736-4509
707-822-9163
www.paracay.com

Contents

Cover Photo courtesy U.S. Coast Guard.

Foreword

During the 505 World Championships in Santa Cruz, California, I was asked to take out members of the yachting press on West Marine's 26 foot lobster boat *Showtime*. As is common in Santa Cruz in the summer, the winds were out of the west at 20 knots, and the swell and wind chop made the ride very uncomfortable. Whenever *Showtime* was put into neutral so the passengers could snap some photographs, she would immediately pivot until she lay a-hull, and would roll back and forth making photography challenging to say the least.

At some point, I remembered that I had a small Para-Tech sea anchor on board, measuring only 6 feet across. Too small to be a legitimate storm sea anchor, it was never-the-less ideal for our purposes. I attached it to *Showtime's* anchor rode and paid out about 100 feet of line. What happened next was remarkable—*Showtime* fetched up on the line, promptly swung her bow around into the wind, and calmed down remarkably. Her pitching was very modest, due to the resistance of the sea anchor on her bow as she passed over each crest, and the relaxation of the rode as she entered the next trough. Not surprisingly, the conditions in the cockpit had changed from windy and uncomfortable to pleasant, since the hull was now aligned with the wind.

While not much of an epic survival story, this was my introduction to drag devices, and I rapidly became a convert.

For the last ten years, I have been a moderator at Safety at Sea Seminars, jointly sponsored by US Sailing, *Cruising World*, and West Marine. The seminars occur all over the country, from Miami, Florida, to Portland, Maine, to Honolulu, Hawaii. It was at one such seminar in 1993 at the Hawaii Yacht Club that I met Earl Hinz. Earl was deeply tanned, wearing shorts and a bright Aloha shirt, with a ready smile. While he had tens of thousands of miles cruising around the Pacific, on sail and power vessels, as well as being an author of many books on seamanship and cruising, he elected to be in the audience that day to learn more about safety than to be a presenter. That was the start of a great friendship which continues to this day

Many of the questions which arise at Safety at Sea Seminars have to do with drag devices. "Should I buy a sea anchor or a drogue?" "Do you deploy a drogue from the stern or the bow?" "How do you retrieve a sea anchor once it is deployed?" "Isn't the rode likely to chafe through?" Participants are fascinated with drag devices perhaps because, like trysails, storm jibs, and life rafts, we rarely encounter (and assiduously avoid!) conditions where such devices can be put to the test. It is the mystery surrounding these devices, combined with a strong hope that these devices may actually save one's boat if caught in a storm at sea, that makes them the subject of so much interest.

Earl Hinz's latest book of *Heavy Weather Tactics Using Sea Anchors and Drogues* examines drag devices in great detail, drawing from his personal observations, information from manufacturers, and reports from users. Rather than being filled with technical jargon, it is eminently practical and readable. All brands of products are dealt with objectively, and a variety of vessel considerations make the book appropriate for power or sail, and monohulls or multihulls. It is an excellent resource for every voyager who has ever wondered "Will I be able to weather the storm I cannot avoid?"

Chuck Hawley
West Marine

Preface

In the thirteen years since my first book on drag devices, *Understanding Sea Anchors & Drogures*, was published, the boating community has seen drag devices come of age as proven options for surviving storms at sea. The early designs have been further refined and new designs have been created giving the offshore sailor more tools with which to combat severe weather. Thousands of boats are carrying drag devices of one sort or another and hundreds of skippers have already used them to enhance their safety in storms as well as to simply improve the ride when the seas became boisterous. Just as the self-steering wind vane or autopilot has given the shorthanded offshore cruiser another crewman to steer his boat, sea anchors and drogues have given the offshore cruiser and racer an alternative means to combat a threatening sea.

With all of the boats sailing the seas and oceans today, we are finding that there is a lot more wild weather than we had expected. Major sailing disasters of recent years (Fastnet 1979, Queen's Birthday Storm 1994, Sydney-Hobart 1998, Nightmare off New Zealand 1998, Carib 1500 1998), have been the result of unexpectedly dangerous weather events rapidly enveloping a fleet in spite of being carefully tracked, analyzed, and reported by competent meteorologists. At best, forecasts can only inform you of developing heavy weather situations along your route, it is up to you to interpret them and select suitable storm tactics. A well-prepared blue water boat should be able to handle all weather in its journey without having to jury-rig a contraption of doubtful performance at the critical moment.

There is a growing trend towards sailing off the beaten path for more adventure; sailing under time restrictions to make port for personal reasons; and also sailing in rallies thinking that there is security in numbers— these are the precursors of danger! The advent of the weather router has lulled many into believing that someone is watching over him (for a price, of course), but one should understand that marine meteorologists have to work with a paucity of data (compared with land meteorologists) because ocean area reporting stations are few and widely scattered. Their forecasts tend more to macro-scale than to micro-scale. Local gales and occasional storms are micro-events, probably not evident in your forecaster's data and even if they were, what can you do about them? All boats, sail or power, are distressingly slow when plowing through heavy seas. As the local weather deteriorates, as the barometer falls, as the seaway builds, it is up to the skipper, not a disembodied voice from space to make the survival decisions. While many vessels have weathered severe storms in the past through good seamanship, we also have to recognize that the thousands of blue water sailors on the oceans today are far less qualified as seamen than the Hiscocks, Smeetons, Griffiths, Roths, et al, of past days. There is a place in modern blue water sailing for drag devices to assist both the neophyte cruiser and the learned seaman in helping bring his boat through a storm.

When it came time to reprint *Understanding Sea Anchors & Drogues*, the author and publisher jointly agreed to let it lie fallow for a few years in view of two other books on the same subject coming on the market—*Drag Device Data Base* by Victor Shane and *The Sea Anchor and Drogue Handbook* by Daniel Shewmon. In a free marketplace this may seem a bit strange, but Victor, Dan and myself have always worked very closely on matters concerning drag devices, the objective not being income, but disseminating information on these unique devices which can enhance boating safety. In fact, I wrote the Preface to the 3rd and 4th editions of Victor's *Drag Device Data Base* and used with Dan's permission data from his book *The Sea Anchor and Drogue Handbook*. Between the three books we covered the stormfront—Victor with a multitude of anecdotal accounts and analysis of drag devices in use, Dan with technical analysis of designs and extensive test results, and myself with an overview on how they work and should be applied.

Interest in drag devices has grown exponentially in recent years as extensive discussions emerged on the Internet and numerous magazine articles appeared written by experts and pseudo-experts on both sailboat and powerboat applications. Sadly, many of the stories were falling back into archaic ideas fostered in earlier years when a sea anchor was anything in the boat's gear inventory you could put overboard without regard to its efficacy or real purpose. I spent hours replying to Internet messages and writing to magazine editors critiquing false concepts that would get boaters in trouble if they followed them. Many of the anecdotal accounts that claimed drag device failure were found to be caused by misapplications, as for instance, using too small a sea anchor; not positioning a drogue the proper distance behind the vessel; and not acknowledging the high loads and chafing problems that are attendant with these devices.

All the while more people were taking to the sea in cruising boats, sailing into parts of the world where few boats had gone before. They were leaving the milk runs to venture into areas little seen by recreational craft in the past. There also grew a tendency to travel in groups with an attendant herd mentality that called for rigid sailing schedules challenging the capabilities of weather services to supply precise weather predictions early enough to allow boats to escape the wrath of the worst weather. As a result, the sailing community was beginning to experience more sailing disasters and with expanding communications, they were being reported on a world wide basis by a news media sensing opportunities for hyping more tales of extreme adventure.

The frame of reference against which most contemporary sailing disasters is measured is the 1979 Fastnet Race which took place off the south coast of England, August 14th, 1979. The 605 mile race had 303 starters, but only 85 finishers. Of the 24 boats which were abandoned, 19 were later recovered, but in the meantime 15 crew members were lost. This event, more than any other in sailing history, served to hasten the development of drag devices as an alternative means of survival when ordinary seamanship cannot do the job.

Other sailing disasters followed and, although drag device technology was well on its way to maturation, yachtsmen still failed to place the devices on board, hence, they were often not available when the chips were down. Extreme weather was still having a field day by way of the 1994 Queen's Birthday Storm northeast of New Zealand which saw seven out of 35 boats abandoned and three crew persons lost in an eighth boat. Crews were mostly couples, who became exhausted applying conventional survival tactics when they did not have drag devices aboard to aid them. About 15 other boats were in passage, but they sailed either before or after the extreme weather cell developed and survived by the luck of the draw.

Extreme weather was still having its way in 1998 and that year will live in sailor's memories for a long time as a trio of racing and cruising fleets from the Atlantic to the Tasman Sea experienced the wrath of Mother Nature. The 1998 West Marine Carib 1500 was assaulted by the tail end of Hurricane Mitch. It managed to sink the 282 foot long tall ship *Fantome* off Honduras and devastate the Honduran countryside with hurricane winds and floods that killed over 10,000 persons. As Mitch tailed off across the Atlantic it intercepted some of the Carib 1500 cruising boats forcing two of them to be abandoned. No lives were loss for which the nine crew members rescued can thank the Coast Guard's quick and efficient response to their EPIRB calls.

A late November 1998 gale off New Zealand tried to replicate the 1994 Queen's Birthday Storm by assaulting a fleet of 30 boats returning to New Zealand from holiday cruises to Fiji, Tonga and New Caledonia. This storm sunk four more cruising boats and cost four lives. The final tragedy of 1998 occurred during the 630 mile Sydney-Hobart race at the end of the year when hurricane force winds coming out of Bass Strait enveloped most of the fleet. Of the 115 boats that started only 39 finished. Six boats were abandoned and six sailors were lost in the rapidly developing storm whose forecast could not keep up with its real life growth.

The foregoing events were organized races, rallies or regattas to which can be added uncounted vessels sailing independently who also suffered extreme storm damage with some never arriving at their intended destinations. They rarely make headlines and just remain mysteries of the sea. This litany of sailing disasters proves that Mother Nature has not changed in her challenge to those "who go down to the sea in ships." While some boat crews have an abundance of experience, others lack heavy weather seamanship skills because time has been limited for them to develop their skills while pursuing lives on land in anticipation of going on an adventure of a lifetime.

Some sailors are so lucky that they are never involved with storms. Others are put to the test while pursuing their adventures and found wanting in seamanship skills. Without adequate seamanship skills and not having a drag device on board when the chips are down, leaves few options other than prayer. The potential benefits of a drag device cannot be realized during a storm unless it is already on board when the boat leaves port. Carrying a drag device on a racing boat seems contrary to the macho psyche considered necessary to win races, yet when expensive race boats and experienced crews can no longer stand up to Mother Nature as in Fastnet 79 and Sydney-Hobart 98, it would be very useful to have an ace in the hole like a drag device to help survival along.

An excerpt from Rob Mundle's exciting story of the fateful 1998 Sidney-Hobart race *(Fatal Storm*, 1999) tells it all:

> Tough little *Canon Maris* was coping admirably with the conditions and was pushing well into Bass Strait by mid-afternoon. While the yacht was handling it under a No. 4 head sail and reefed mizzen and was in second position on handicap, (owner) Ian Kearnan was annoyed with himself. If conditions worsened, it might be safest to set a sea anchor and ride out the storm. ... But modern race yachts don't carry such cumbersome equipment. ... "I realized I'd forgotten some of the good things that I'd learned about seamanship with this yacht over the years," Kearnan recalls. "I used to carry an old car tire for a sea anchor (sic) and 50-60 fathoms of heavy polypropylene line. ..."

The many instances reported over recent years in which drag devices could have aided in survival or, at least, made the passage more satisfying, convinced me to take *Understanding Sea Anchors & Drogues* out of mothballs and rewrite much of it. The rewrite would focus on new technology in the field and the wealth of experience accumulated in using drag devices as survival aids when the weather turns sour. It is no longer Captain Voss's homemade canvas cone trailing from *Tillicum*, but well-engineered and tested devices made of high tech materials and accepted by knowing sailors for improving heavy weather survivability.

This book is written for blue water sailors who need to understand what drag devices are, how they work, how they should be deployed, and what the potential benefits are. A dedicated skipper with the welfare of his crew in mind will study all aspects of drag devices and make a conscious decision on how well he wants to be prepared for heavy weather. A drag device on board offers him one more way to survive the challenge of the sea when he is wholly on his own.

Acknowledgments

This book is not the work of only one person for it draws on the observations of many persons over many years. Among those who have knowingly (or unknowingly) made contributions to this assessment of sea anchors and drogues are Captain Voss, Fritz Fenger, Robert Manry, the Casanovas, Eric Hiscock, Frank Robb, Harry Pidgeon, Adlard Coles, Ross Norgrove, Robin Knox-Johnston, William Van Dorn, the Pardeys, Bernard Moitessier, and Bob Griffith to name the more familiar ones. Through their experiences, and writings by and about them, the boating world has learned much about seamanship under adverse conditions. And we should not forget the many crewmen who participated in the disastrous Fastnet Race of 1979 which first proved the need for new heavy weather survival techniques. Thanks to John Rousmaniere for so completely documenting this tragic event in his book *Fastnet, Force 10*.

The author also wishes to give recognition to state-of-the-art contributions made to drag devices by Dan Shewmon and Donald Jordan through their technical articles in *Cruising World* and *Sail* magazines, respectively. These lively forums have brought forth most of the problems of, and many solutions to, small boat storm survival.

Thanks is also due to several manufacturers for their unstinting cooperation in sharing development experiences on drag devices—Skip Raymond of Hathaway, Reiser & Raymond, Dan Shewmon of Shewmon, Inc., and Don Whillden of Para-Tech Engineering Co. They have been in the front line of the evolution of a new generation of survival gear.

I owe a personal debt of gratitude to Victor Shane for the opportunity of being able to work with him during his preparation of the 4th edition of the *Drag Device Data Base*. The breadth of real world experiences covered in his book served to identify many important design and performance characteristics of sea anchors and drogues essential to understanding how they work.

Although there is certainly no technical relationship involved between the world of high tech computing devices and drag devices, it was a happy coincidence that their early evolutionary periods coincided. For one, the advent of Internet forums provided almost daily debates on the merits of drag devices and other heavy weather survival techniques. New ideas and first hand experiences were heard and weighed. Thanks, sailors from around the world, your postings have been read and considered herein.

A second contribution came from Publisher Matt Morehouse who applied the latest techniques in Publishing to bring this new book out of the ancestral world of cut-and-paste publishing used with the former *Understanding Sea Anchors & Drogues*. Susan Vogt efficiently put copy, artwork and photographs together on a single "floppy" for me easing my task of bringing this expanded millennial edition on drag devices into the 21st century. Thanks Matt and Susan for being so progressive.

Finally, I again had the talents of Dick Rhodes for the illustrations. He had also done the illustrations for my book *The Complete Book of Anchoring and Mooring*. Read about him in the end papers.

Yesterday

And now the STORM-BLAST came, and he
Was tyrannous and strong;
He struck with his o'ertaking wings,
And chased us south along.

With sloping masts and dipping prow,
As who pursued with yell and blow
Still treads the shadow of his foe,
And forward bends his head,
The ship drove fast, loud roared the blast,
And southward aye we fled.
Samuel T. Coleridge, *The Rime of the Ancient Mariner*

1

Today

"The Committee's investigation into drogues, sea anchors and parachute sea anchors or a makeshift alternative, shows their use would have been a sound option in the conditions of the 1998 race."

Cruising Yacht Club of Australia Race Review Committee

CHAPTER ONE

Sea Anchor or Drogue?

The use of drag devices at sea has been fraught with confusion, contradiction, and controversy. Confusion over what the difference is between a sea anchor and a drogue; contradiction on what constitutes a proper design; and controversy on how and when to use them or whether to use them at all. They do have a place in the survival equipment inventory of recreational and working blue water boats, but first we have to take a hard look at what has gone before that has caused the indeterminate state of affairs.

Sea anchors have been around a long time, indicating that early seafarers also felt the need to "stop" the boat for crew comfort and to keep the bow into the wind for survival. There is some evidence that early Polynesian seafarers (circa 1200 AD) used a form of sea anchor on their double-hulled voyaging canoes. This was done by attaching stone ground anchors to sennit (coconut fiber) ropes and lowering them from the bows of the canoe hulls. Supposedly this brought the bows into the wind so that the shallow draft canoes could ride out the storm with greater ease. Since the canoes were steered with long dismountable oars, there was no tendency to break the rudder in a sudden rearward movement of the canoe.

Webster's dictionary notes that the first use of the term "sea anchor" in recorded English writing occurred in 1769. The word "drogue", however, did not appear in English writings until 1875 and it is believed to have started as a variant of the word "drag."

The first well-documented account of using sea anchors and drogues came from Captain John Voss's book on his voyages in the Pacific in a converted British Columbia Indian canoe (Voss 1949). On several occasions Voss found it advantageous to rig a conical sea anchor from the bow of *Tilikum* to ride out a storm. There are several features of *Tilikum* which made it a suitable vessel for sea anchoring. First, it was a narrow-beamed boat of shallow draft. Second, it did not have great windage forward nor a large keel aft that would have tended to turn it broadside to the wind and waves. Lastly, it had a removable rudder, at least it was removable after Voss found out on two occasions that the backward motion of the boat could break the rudder. On the third sea anchor deployment, Voss unshipped the rudder and there was no further trouble.

Even then *Tilikum* did not lie perfectly head to sea but held a position about 5 points (approximately 55°) off the wind. Voss then added a leg-o'-mutton spanker sheeted in flat and cut the riding angle down one-half. Voss claims to have "weathered sixteen gales without shipping so much as a bucket of water at one time."

That same drag device that performed so successfully as a sea anchor was also used as a drogue in crossing the dangerous bar at Melbourne, Australia, and later in a demonstration of towing a boat across a bar at Whanganui, New Zealand.

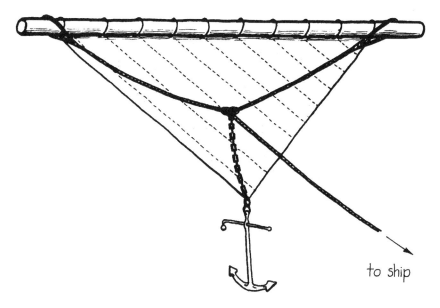

to ship

The drift sail. The earliest attempts at sea anchoring in the western world took place in the 17th century with what was then called a drift sail. It was made from a spar with sail attached. An anchor was hung from the clew of the sail with a length of chain connecting the clew to a rope bridle coming from the other corners. The hawser was knotted to the three-part bridle and the bitter end attached to the ship. Adapted from *The Mariner's Dictionary*.

Specifications for building the Voss sea anchors are given in his book and two examples are illustrated in Figure 1.

Anyone who was interested in sea anchors (or drogues) continued to use the Voss conical device until 1932 when Fritz Fenger put his analytical and mechanical mind to work in developing a new concept. Out of his experiments came the "double plank drogue." Fenger's design (*Yachting*, January 1968) was sturdy, heavy, and awkward to stow, but it worked well as either a sea anchor or a drogue—so it is said. Figure 2 is a design worked up for a boat with a 35-foot waterline. The weight of this device is approximately 55 pounds in air.

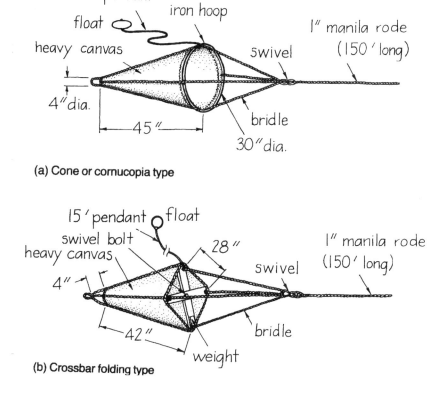

(a) Cone or cornucopia type

(b) Crossbar folding type

Figure 1. Sea anchors according to Voss (dimensions given for a deep keel boat with 30-foot waterline.)

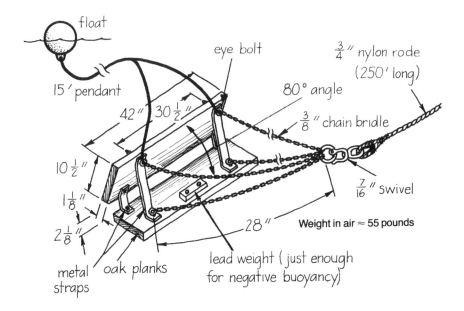

Figure 2. Fenger-type drogue for 35-foot-waterline boat.

Apparently sea anchors continued to be carried by some blue water boats but little was written about them. Most cruisers still did not have faith in them although many kept them on board just in case everything else failed. Next to use one was Robert Manry in 1965 during a gale while crossing the Atlantic in the 13 1/2-foot-long *Tinkerbelle*. His only problem was that the boat would not lie bow to the wind until he had unshipped the transom-mounted rudder. *Tinkerbelle* then rode comfortably head to the wind (Manry 1966).

Later proponents of the sea anchor are John and Joan Casanova who are devotees of the parachute sea anchor. They have successfully used what they term the "parachute anchoring system" on their trimaran *Tortuga Too*. *Tortuga Too* rode to a parachute sea anchor many times when gales set in during her 33,000-mile circumnavigation. John says, "Never wait until the last minute to put out the chute. Watch your bad weather signs. When you become nervous and a bit concerned, it is time to use the parachute and go below; relax if you can." (Casanova et al. 1982)

But not everybody had the same feelings about sea anchors and drogues. Reading through the literature of cruising one finds that Eric Hiscock had used one (a drogue) and believed it to be an "essential piece of gear...enabling [a boat] to ride out the worst kind of weather in safety and by reducing her drift to a minimum, keeping her off a lee shore." He also found out that a good drogue had to be stronger than the traditional canvas sea anchor since his was essentially shredded by the time it was hauled aboard (Hiscock 1956).

Frank Robb also had drogue experience and says that they "have many vices and only one virtue—they check drift." (*Sea*, January 1979)

And Hal Roth, a blue water sailor of much experience, says, "The theory of a yachtsman's sea anchor is...to hold the ship's head to the wind and expose the strongest and most streamlined part to the vessel to the storm...This is a nice fairy tale, which, unfortunately, is nonsense."

Harry Pidgeon carried a sea anchor made out of some "boards" on his shakedown cruise between Los Angeles and Hawaii in 1921, but there is no evidence that he ever used his contraption. After that cruise he made a new sea anchor out of canvas which he took along on his world cruise.

Pidgeon had no occasion to use his new sea anchor until early in 1924, when he departed Durban, South Africa. The Agulhas current carried him steadily south but soon head winds turned into a westerly gale on the Agulhas bank and he hove-to under reefed mizzen and storm jib. The combers of the wild sea would drive the bow off and slew *Islander* almost beam-on. After the storm jib split, he put out the sea anchor, but alas, it apparently had been designed after Voss's recommendations and *Islander* was in no way a *Tilikum*. Pidgeon said, "It [the sea anchor] appeared to be too light to sink to the proper depth and was not large enough." So Pidgeon set about repairing the split storm jib and later rode out the rest of the storm hove-to (Pidgeon 1954).

Ross Norgrove tried a Fenger drogue once and proved the difference between a sea anchor and a drogue. In his book *The Cruising Life* he describes using a 5-foot-span Fenger-type drogue streamed on 100 fathoms of 5/8-inch-diameter rope from the bow of *White Squall* in a Roaring Forties gale. The response of the boat was to lie beam-on in the trough. As she would rise up on the face of one wave, the bow would start to swing downwind and the shoulder of the boat would take the punch of the next wave. He felt a lesser-built boat would not have survived the pounding.

Nevertheless, enough was enough and even if the boat was taking these shoulder punches, the crew could not. So Norgrove brought 50 feet of the sea anchor warp outside of everything and made it fast to the aft Samson post. Then the warp was freed from the forward Samson post, *White Squall* quickly turned end for end and took a more comfortable position with the sea. His final observation was, "Upon reflection, I would say that without that wooden contraption over the stern, or something equally as good, we would not have been anywhere near as safe."

Norgrove later encountered a true sea anchor in use by a 50-foot ex-Bluenose schooner. It was a 25-foot-diameter parachute that was capable of holding the schooner's nose into a 25-knot wind. While he thought this was the answer to a seaman's prayer, he still had reservations about holding the boat too securely when it may have been better turning and running with a drogue (Norgrove 1980).

Much of the confusion and contradiction on sea anchors and drogues can be traced back to John Voss's book *The Venturesome Voyages of Captain Voss*, in which he relates his experiences with sea anchors on *Tilikum*. He used the same drag device over the bow for a sea anchor as he used over the stern to run a bar and he always called it a sea anchor (Voss 1949).

Henderson, writing in *Sea Sense* (1979), makes a nominal difference between the drag devices:

> Sometimes a distinction is made between a drogue and a sea anchor but essentially each is a floating anchor designed to slow a vessel's drift and to hold her in a desired attitude. We could differentiate between the two to some extent by saying that the sea anchor is intended to reduce drift to a bare minimum, while the drogue is merely a drag to lessen drift.

Another piece of contemporary literature defines a sea anchor as follows:

> **SEA ANCHOR:** Any object or collection of objects streamed to windward to slow down the leeward rush of a vessel in heavy weather. A true sea anchor is a canvas open-ended cone which is streamed on the end of line from a bridle. Under practical conditions the sea anchor tends to be insufficient or it readily carries away. One of the best alternatives is a collection of floorboards, fenders and tires lashed together and streamed. Long bights of rope and chain with nothing attached can also serve to slow the vessel down.

Even dictionaries do not offer a clear, concise differentiation between the two drag devices. *Webster's Collegiate Dictionary* published by Random House in 1992 says:

> **sea anchor**: any of various devices, as a drogue, that are dropped at the end of a cable to hold the bow of a vessel into the wind.
> **drogue**: **1**: a bucket or a canvas bag used as a sea anchor. **2.a**: a funnel-shaped device attached to the end of a hose on a tanker aircraft for connecting with the probe of another airplane to be refueled in flight. **b**: a small parachute that is deployed in order to open a large parachute.

Although the dictionary's definition of the term "sea anchor" approximates its current usage, that for a drogue (in maritime use) only muddies the waters by referring to it as a sea anchor. This is the Voss syndrome all over again.

There is a need for consistent definitions of these two drag devices that have received a bum rap in the past when drogues were used over the bow and had virtually no capability of bringing the bow of the boat into the wind. It is important to differentiate between them because they are physically quite different and they perform different functions.

Confusion would reign on a boat if you did not differentiate between a halyard and a sheet; or between a spring line and a breast line; or between a genoa and a staysail. Yet all of these parts of a boat have great similarity in appearances, but are used differently.

A *sea anchor* is a large drag device deployed over the *bow* of a boat to hold the bow into the wind and the wave. It has to be large enough to prevent the bow from falling off and allowing the boat to lie broadside to the waves. A boat riding to a sea anchor will experience some leeward drift depending on the relative size of the sea anchor and the boat and the fury of the storm. A proper sea anchor will hold the backward drift to under 1 or 2 knots maximum. To allow the boat to drift aft at a greater speed is to put the rudder at risk. A sea anchor is used when a boat is disabled or the crew no longer wishes to sail, but would simply like to hold a relatively safe position and attitude with respect to the seas.

A *drogue* is a smaller drag-producing device that is deployed over the *stern* of a boat to slow its forward progress when running downwind and, to some extent, to hold the stern to the seas. In general, the drag of a drogue is considerably less than that of a sea anchor; hence, the forward speed of a boat towing a drogue will be considerably greater than the backward speed of a sea-anchored boat. When using a drogue (series drogue excepted), rudder control must be maintained so a compatible boat speed must be preserved. This may be as high as 5 or 10 knots and probably never less than 3 knots. A drogue is used when the crew feels that it is necessary to slow the forward progress of the boat while running downwind without surrendering control to the elements and while there is plenty of sea room to safely continue progress.

The differences in deployment of these two drag devices are illustrated in Figure 3.

William Van Dorn, in his book *Oceanography and Seamanship* (1974), says, "Of all common safety items, sea anchors (or drogues) have probably received the least engineering attention, as is well borne out by the variability of reports from those who have tried using them." But this situation has changed greatly since his writing. Shewmon, Inc., of Safety Harbor, Florida, has been engaged for a number of years in developing and testing sea anchors and drogues. Engineering design products have been subjected to extensive tugboat pull-testing before being put on the market. Para-Tech Engineering of Silt, Colorado, has transferred the airman's parachute technology to sea anchors and drogues. Hathaway, Reiser & Raymond of Stamford, Connecticut, has created an exceptionally novel drogue that was given the acid test in a Gulf Stream storm and came out with flying colors. Donald Jordan, an aeronautical engineer under the sponsorship of the US Coast Guard, conducted extensive studies into the nature of breaking waves and their effects on boats. Out of it came the revolutionary series drogue concept.

What has prompted this long overdue development activity in boat drag devices? In general it is due to the large increase in the number of boaters that are exposing themselves to Nature's fury while fishing, sailing, racing, and cruising. The need for this type of equipment has grown and it is now recognized as a viable product in the marketplace.

Even more than the general growth of boating was the impact of the 1979 Fastnet Race disaster when 24 boats either sank or were abandoned and 15 lives lost when a severe gale passed through the fleet. It is fantasy to conjecture whether any of those lives could have been saved if the boats had been equipped with sea anchors and/or drogues. We do know, though, that one boat, *Windswept*, did deploy a drogue and survived the event in spite of serious damage and crew injuries. Most of the reasons given later for crews having abandoned boats—dismastings, loss of rudders, capsizing, and intolerable motions below decks—are conditions which often can be alleviated through the use of either a sea anchor or a drogue.

The use of a drag device should be considered when winds and seas cause the helmsman's knuckles to turn white. Common sense at some point must overrule macho determination to complete a race or a passage. Van Dorn offers two quantitative measures of when to consider your vessel in danger from the seas: The first is when the wave height nears a match with the width of the vessel's beam. At that point it is dangerous to take the seas beam-on. To continue sailing across the wind is to invite a capsize or, even worse, a 360° roll. The second measure applies when the wave height nears a match with the vessel's length. At that point, pitchpoling of the boat becomes a distinct possibility.

It is critical to the well-being of the boat and crew for the skipper to

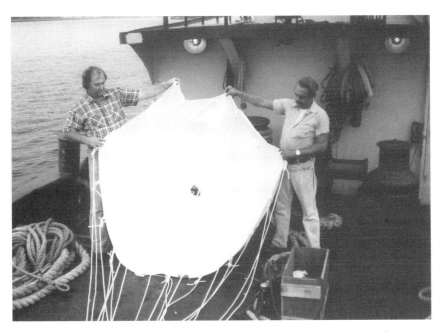

A 6-foot-diameter Mark III Shewmon sea anchor on the aft deck of a harbor tug used in the testing program. Courtesy Shewmon, Inc.

wind

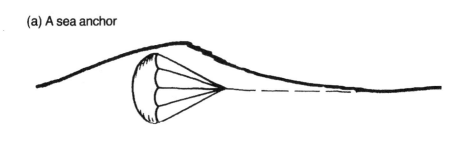

(a) A sea anchor

wave direction

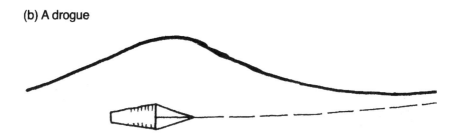

(b) A drogue

Figure 3. Using drag devices in a storm.

make tactical decisions to ward off potential disaster when the wave height reaches the width of the boat's beam. Possible tactics would involve the use of a sea anchor or a drogue to keep the boat aligned with waves either bow-on or stern-on with speed moderated.

Heaving-to or lying a-hull in waves of lesser height than one beam width has been a successful tactic for many years. Heaving-to or lying a-hull when the waves reach or exceed one beam width in height would seem to be courting disaster, especially when they are breaking. If there can be any argument here, it is only in estimating wave height under adverse circumstances. For those who may think their vessels are impervious to Van Dorn's rule of thumb, tank tests (Jordan, *Sail* magazine, June 1986, September 1984, December 1982, and February 1982) and numerous actual experiences (e.g., the 1979 Fastnet Race) seem to verify the rule.

In the 1979 Fastnet Race it was the smaller boats which were capsized or pitchpoled, indicating at least a qualitative relationship between boat size and wave height. Since the waves were so large and confused, there was no way to relate the boat's beam or length to wave height. Conditions were well beyond that simple relationship. One boat in the 44- to 55-foot class had to be abandoned, but otherwise the casualties occurred in the classes 38 feet in length and less (Rousmaniere 1980).

One use for the sea anchor (not the drogue) for which there is little argument is the situation where the vessel is faced with being blown onto a lee shore. While there remains a safe sea distance, a large sea anchor set to windward will give the boat a new lease on life and the crew an opportunity to solve the problem of how to escape the lee shore. The few hundred dollars that the skipper invested in a proper sea anchor could be the sweetest insurance he ever purchased.

Probably the most common reason for carrying a sea anchor is to stabilize the boat in case of a major failure short of sinking. In the event that a powerboat loses its primary propulsion, a deployed sea anchor (not a drogue) will keep its bow into the waves and permit repairs to be made to the power plant. There is no comparison to the ease of working inside a boat when it is bow to the waves rather than rolling in a trough.

Maximum comfort and a measure of safety in heavy seas can only be found on a boat when the bow is pointed into the waves and the roll is reduced to a minimum. That is the domain of the sea anchor.

For the blue water sailor who is racing or cruising, the value of sea anchors and drogues in common mishaps should not be underestimated. Take the case of a dismasting, or blown sails, or a broken rudder. To lie helpless without propulsion or steerage is a fate worse than death—an unwelcome, very possible alternative if the 1979 Fastnet Race is any indication.

Take, for instance, the saga of *Ipo*, a 30-foot sloop out of Honolulu that departed Lahaina, Maui, for her home port in forecasted mild weather. Soon after departure, the weather changed for the worse. A whole gale descended from the north catching the boat with all sails standing and tearing mainsail and jib beyond repair. With no other sails on board, the skipper of *Ipo* decided to motor back into port, only to find that the iron genny was also under the weather. Now there was nothing to do but radio for help, for the north wind was blowing *Ipo* away from the islands and the next stop would have been Palmyra atoll, 1,000 miles south. The Coast Guard, as they do so often, saved the day and brought *Ipo* into port.

It is conceivable that a sea anchor could have helped in *Ipo*'s situation. Having it hold the bow to the seas when the engine failed may have allowed the crew to make essential repairs to get the engine started. Certainly a sea anchor would have reduced the drift of the boat, which was over 60 miles in 24 hours. While double propulsion failures (sails and engine) are rare, nevertheless, the sea anchor makes sense for self sufficiency.

The drogue comes into its own on still-functioning boats when it is desired to continue sailing downwind and downwave. A drogue set over the stern can moderate the speed to a controllable level as well as to hold the stern into the waves to prevent broaching. It can, in fact, stop the boat if it is a series drogue, but that is another subject taken up later.

Sailors racing modern light displacement sailboats find that in gale conditions it is often better to turn downwind and keep the boat sailing rather than fighting to windward, lying a-hull, or heaving-to. The problem then becomes one of keeping the boat's speed under control, as light displacement boats easily pick up speed on the waves and like to go surfing. As a boat's speed approaches wave speed (10 to 20 knots) there is a great danger of loss of control resulting in broaching or pitchpoling. Either spells disaster. But there is a solution—a drogue over the stern to moderate the boat's speed without stopping it. A proper drogue will still allow the boat to sail fast downwind but it will be under better control and will give the helmsman more time to make corrections as the overtaking seas change shape and direction.

Thomas Seabrook in critiquing survival tactics used in the Fastnet Race said (*Yacht Racing/Cruising*, February 1983):

> Boats whose skippers chose to lie a-hull under bare poles and therefore were unable to take action to avoid particularly dangerous seas were worse off than those that were kept under speed and steering control. The strong consensus among skippers was that the helm should be manned at all times. From this it would seem active rather than passive tactics will be more successful during a severe storm.

In another application a drogue can be very useful when running river mouths or inlets to harbors where sand bars create short, steep waves. If you absolutely must run a bar that is breaking, your chances of successfully doing so are immeasurably improved if a proper drogue is deployed before the entrance is reached. Once you enter the waters of the bar, your fate is in the hands of the helmsman, the drogue, and the Almighty.

Like all anchoring skills, practice is essential to the proper deployment of a drag device, be it a sea anchor or a drogue. The environment is at its worst when the need arises, and that is no time to learn correct deployment procedures. If you have practiced your sea anchor and drogue deployment under less pressing circumstances, the chances are that you can make a proper deployment when the seas are up.

After an extensive review of the literature on sea anchors, drogues, and storm survival, and after having talked with many persons on the subject, I believe that bad experiences with these devices have been the result of improper use. On the other hand, the proper use of a drag device has time and again shown itself as a way to storm survival.

It is not within the scope of this book to get into the broader subject of other tactics to be used during heavy weather. The reader is referred to K. Adlard Cole's book, *Heavy Weather Sailing* (1996), *Storm Tactics Handbook* (1995) by Lin and Larry Pardey and *Surviving the Storm* (1999) by Steve and Linda Dashew for discussions on heaving-to, lying a-hull, running at high speeds, and other survival techniques applicable to medium to heavy displacement boats. For light displacement boats the reader is referred to John Rousmaniere's book, *Fastnet, Force 10* (1980), which describes in vivid detail the techniques used by several racing sailboats to survive what was the most disastrous racing event in the history of the sport.

If you, the potential offshore sailor, need convincing evidence about the value of carrying drag devices on your otherwise well-found boat, you will find it in the pages of the *Drag Device Data Base* (Shane 1998). Herein are first hand, real life experiences of those who have survived the "ultimate storm" through the use of drag devices. Read these case histories (120 of them) and then rearrange your equipment priorities. You stand to become the beneficiary and not your heirs.

Shed all sailors' tales when you read the present book and think objectively about the differences between sea anchors and drogues. Then you will be prepared to choose the drag device that offers the best chance for survival when you encounter your own ultimate storm.

CHAPTER TWO

Deep Water Wave Characteristics

Contrary to what might be the first thoughts by sailors, it is not the wind that is damaging in heavy weather situations but the waves. Of course you will be right in saying that the wind created the waves in the first place, but it is the response of your vessel to the waves that is important. When you have totally down-powered your boat, there is little wind left to directly effect your boat's safety and the comfort of the crew provided that you have chosen an appropriate survival tactic for the current conditions. Maybe you have chosen to heave-to, which means using the wind with a minimum of sails to smooth out your turbulent ride over the seas. Or, you have chosen to use a sea anchor and raise a small sail aft to aid in holding the boat's bow comfortably into the wind. Or you have chosen to run with the wind and you have raised a small headsail to assure the boat will head downwind at the best speed with or without a drogue. In any event, the wind is only used to support your survival tactic against the wave action which it has caused. It can, indeed, become dangerous in a storm's life if you have fully down-powered or the wind has quit with the seas still turbulent, then with little or no wind damping of the wave-induced rolling motion of the boat, a capsize becomes a possibility.

Following are some thoughts to keep in mind as you read this chapter on deep water wave characteristics:

- Changes in the seas are more critical to the small craft than to a sailing ship, as for instance, confused seas, crossing seas, and rogue waves
- The shape of the waves is more important than the strength of the wind
- The shape of the wave deteriorates rapidly from the theoretical sinusoidal shape to simple chaos
- It is difficult to estimate wave heights above those which have been

personally observed in the past
- Waves are potentially destructive to any vessel in any body of water

ANATOMY OF DEEP WATER WAVES

Waves come in three different forms—ripples, gravity waves and swells—all caused by the wind. Combinations of the three are occasionally referred to as a "seaway." Ripples appear first on smooth waters when light winds begin to blow and they die quickly with no after effects when the wind dies. Ripples are capillary waves whose restoring force is the water's surface tension. These are the familiar catspaws sought after in sailing races when winds are Beaufort Force 0 or 1.

Gravity waves are created by a building or constant significant wind —winds from Beaufort 2 and up. They have a more pronounced form and live a longer life than ripples even after the wind has ceased.

Swells are waves that have been generated by wind in another geographic area and are unrelated to the local winds. They are in fact waves that have outlasted their generating winds. As far as boats are concerned, swells have little direct effect on them, but when combined with large gravity waves, they can produce extreme seaways. Swells are not as sharply defined as waves, being of greater length and somewhat lesser height:

Swell length (distance crest to crest)
Short swell	0 to 325 feet
Average swell	325 to 650 feet
Long swell	over 650 feet

Swell height (average of well-formed swell waves)
Low swell	0 to 6 1/2 feet
Moderate swell	6 1/2 to 13 feet
Heavy swell	over 13 feet

In general, swells travel at 300 to 500 miles per day with the longest wavelengths traveling the fastest. Changes in swell patterns may be the first sign of an oncoming wind change (if not caused by nearby land.)

It will be seen later that the water in waves and swells does not travel anyplace, it merely sits in one place and moves up and down in a rhythm that makes it appear to be moving.

NON-BREAKING WAVES

Gravity waves in deep water (water depth which is greater than one-half the wave length) are generated by the wind and their shape is unaffected by the proximity of the bottom.

Sine wave

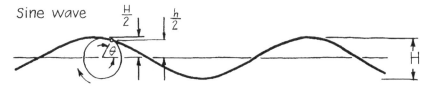

The sine wave is generated by plotting the vertical height above and below a horizontal line of a point on the rim of a rotating wheel. As the wheel rotates, the height varies as the trigonometic function: $\frac{h}{2} = \frac{H}{2} \sin \theta$.

trochoidal wave

The trochoidal wave is generated by a wheel rolling along the underside of a line, with a fixed point on one spoke tracing the wave shape.

cycloidal wave

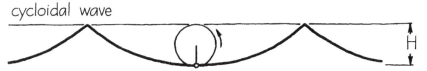

The cycloidal wave is created in a manner similar to the trochoidal wave, except that the point generating the wave is at the rim of the wheel.

Figure 4. Mathematical representations of deep water wave shapes.

The general shape of a wave at low wind speeds is that of a mathematical sine wave. As the wind increases in strength, the shape changes to a trochoid and then to a cycloid at wind speeds approaching 60 knots. Over 60 knots the seas become so confused that simple mathematical representations no longer make sense. Let us take a look at the sinusoidal wave form in order to develop our language of waves.

We see in Figure 5 a simple wave shape with representations of wave length L, wave height H, and depth of water D. The crests are the "hills" of

the wave and the troughs are the "valleys" of the wave. The water is sufficiently deep that there is no influence of the bottom on the wave shape.

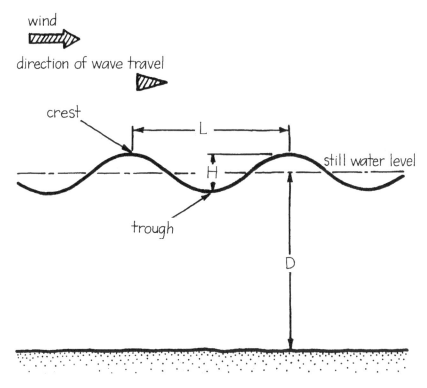

Figure 5. Deep water wave characteristics

Wave heights are very difficult to measure in the real sea. Bowditch
in the *American Practical Navigator* has developed a wave height scale
that corresponds with the wind speeds on the Beaufort scale. (Beaufort
wind speeds are measured at 10 meters (33 feet) above the sea level.) This
is reproduced in Table 1.

The storm conditions we are particularly interested in are those for
Beaufort Number 7 and above. For those winds we see that wave heights
start at 13 feet and grow to phenomenal heights of over 45 feet. Few of us
will ever see a hurricane at sea, but Beaufort Force 10 (whole gales) are not
uncommon for the blue water cruiser or the long distance ocean racer.

Besides the height of a wave, the motion of the water particles at or
near the surface can be very important to the proper use of sea anchors or

Beaufort number	Wind speed knots	Seaman's term	Estimating wind speed Effects observed at sea	Term and heigth of wave ft*	Sea state code
0	under 1	Calm	Sea like mirror.	Calm, glassy, 0	0
1	1-3	Light air	Ripples with appearance of scales; no foam crests.		
2	4-6	Light breeze	Small wavelets; crests of glassy appearance, not breaking.	Rippled, 0-1	1
3	7-10	Gentle breeze	Large wavelets; crests begin to break; scattered whitecaps.	Wavelets, 1-2	2
4	11-16	Moderate breeze	Small waves, becoming longer; numerous whitecaps.	Slight, 2-4	3
5	17-21	Fresh breeze	Moderate waves, taking longer form; many whitecaps; some spray.	Moderate, 4-8	4
6	22-27	Strong breeze	Larger waves forming; whitecaps everywhere; more spray.	Rough, 8-13	5
7	28-33	Moderate gale	Sea heaps up; white foam from breaking waves begins to be blown in streaks.	Very rough, 13-20	6
8	34-40	Fresh gale	Moderately high waves of greater length; edges of crests begin to break into spin-drift; foam is blown in well-marked streaks.		
9	41-47	Strong gale	High waves; sea begins to roll; dense streaks of foam; spray may reduce visibility.		
10	48-55	Whole gale	Very high waves with overhanging crests; sea takes white appearance as foam is blown in very dense streaks; rolling is heavy and visibility reduced.	High, 20-30	7
11	56-63	Storm	Exceptionally high waves; sea covered with white foam patches; visibility still more reduced.	Very high 30-45	8
12	64-71	Hurricane	Air filled with foam; sea completely white with driving spray; visibility greatly reduced.	Phenomenal over 45	9

Table 1. Wave heights by the Beaufort scale, from Bowditch.

*For a fully developed sea state.

drogues. We have been told that the water near the surface of a wave does not move forward with the wave, only up and down. That is sufficiently correct for a general understanding of waves but not sufficiently exact for designing a sea anchor system for survival. Actually, particles of water within a wave rotate in an orbit at any location, going up and down and forward and backward as the wave passes by. This orbital motion is illustrated in Figure 6.

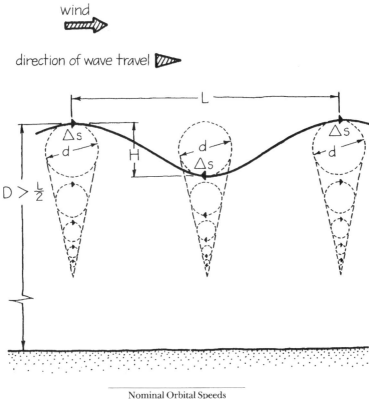

Figure 6. Orbital movement of water particles in a deep water wave.

The diameter d of the orbit is equal to the height H of the wave, and the speed is such that a complete revolution of a particle takes place in a time equal to the period P of the wave. The period of the wave is the time it takes one full wave (from crest to crest) to pass a particular point in space. This orbital motion of water particles extends downward as far as one wave length in depth, but for all practical purposes it has vanished at a depth equal to one-half a wave length. From this relationship we can define deep water as water depth in excess of one-half a wave length for the particular fully developed wave system of interest. If the water is of lesser depth, then bottom effects become noticeable, making the waves steeper and closer together. These types of waves are more appropriate for surfboards than for boats.

There are some basic, deep water wave characteristics which are of interest to us for determining the lengths of sea anchor or drogue rodes as a function of wave length. These are the period, length, speed, and height of the wave as well as the orbital speed of the water particles at the wave surface. The following mathematical relationships describe the wave motion of interest to us:

Length of a wave: $L = 5.12\ P^2$ or $S^2 / 1.8$ [*Equation 1*]

Speed of a wave: $S = 1.36\ L^{1/2}$ or $S = 3.03\ P$ [*Equation 2*]

Orbital speed of a particle: $\Delta s = 1.9\ H/P$ [*Equation 3*]

        where L = wave length (feet)

                   P = wave period (seconds)

                   S = wave speed (knots)

                   Δs = particle orbital speed (knots)

                   H = wave height (feet)

Numerical values of the foregoing deep water relationships can be extracted from tables in *Bowditch* or other oceanographic references.

Besides wind speed the temperature of the air in a weather front can influence breaker development. Warm air moving over a body of water tends to rise and does not impress its movement on the water as much as cold air. A cold front moving across a body of water tends to descend increasing its frictional influence on the water and inspiring the waves to break earlier.

The height of waves is primarily dependent on three factors: wind speed, length of time the wind has been blowing, and the fetch or distance over open water that the wind has been blowing.

Figure 7(a) relates the significant wave height in storms to the wind speeds in Beaufort Force numbers and the duration of the blow in hours. It takes a measurable time for the wind to whip up the seas which is all the time you will have to down-power the boat and prepare your drag device for the worst to come, namely, the full waves that the gale will develop. Move fast for when the full gale-induced waves have arrived, you will be too tired to get ready and will have lost the ease of working in more mod-

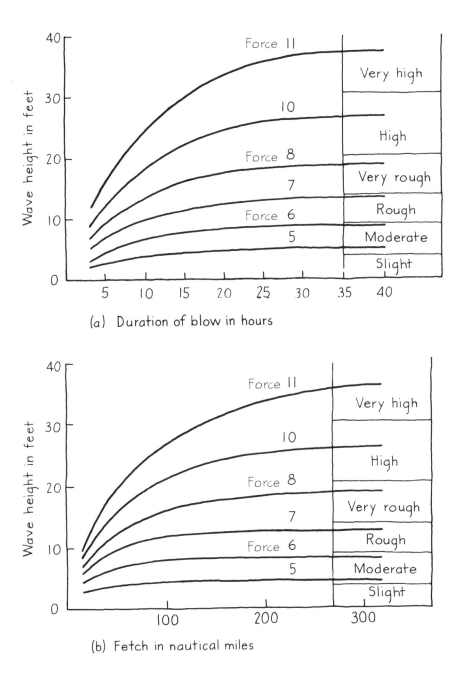

Figure 7. Wave heights generated in steady state blows.

erate wave conditions.

If you have any chance of seeking shelter when the storm is forecast, think of getting into the lee of land to reduce the fetch. Figure 7(b) shows that within about 50 miles of land the wave heights due to gale winds are only about half of what they are a few hundred miles offshore. In suspected gale weather it is worthwhile to plan passages along leeward coasts wherever possible. Blue water sailors have no such opportunity and must be prepared to face the storms. That isn't all bad since they will also have no coastal hazards to worry about.

It is difficult to estimate wave heights above those which have been personally observed in the past. An experienced eye and some height reference must be employed. The modern Beaufort scale lists wave heights as a function of the Beaufort number and an equivalent wind speed. These wave heights represent the effects of a wind that has been blowing continuously for some time over a long fetch to allow full development of waves consistent with the wind speed.

When a weather forecast is received, the wave heights will be given in terms of the "significant wave height" which is the average height of the highest 1/3rd of the waves. The heights of the remaining 2/3rds of the waves will consist of a mix which are related to the significant wave height by the ratios:

Wave height	*Relative height ratio*
Most frequent wave height	.5 : 1
Average wave height	.64 : 1
Significant height	1 : 1
Highest 10 percent	1.29 : 1
Highest (one in a thousand)	1.87 : 1

The spectrum of wave heights is illustrated in Figure 8. These represent ideal waves from one direction only. Storm seas, however, tend to be very confused with waves coming from more than one direction and the granddaddy of waves, the rogue wave, is generated by intersecting strong wave trains whose heights and periods are a matter for conjecture.

One of the conclusions which has come out of the investigation of the 1998 Sydney-Hobart Race (*CYCA*, 1999) tragedy was "that there was a wide gap in understanding between the Bureau of Meteorology scientists'

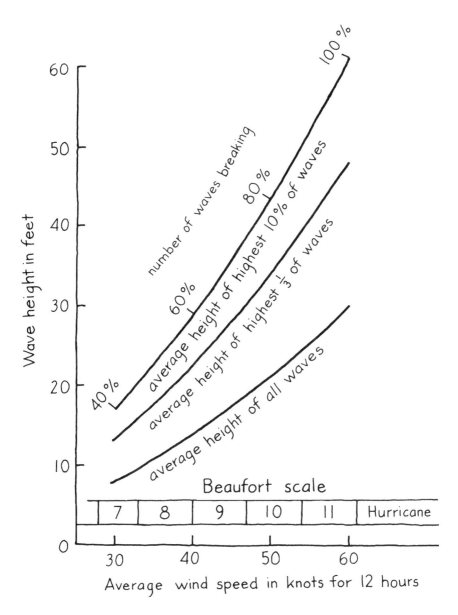

Figure 8. Wind wave height spectrum

forecasting and the interpretation of their forecasts on yachts." This was confirmed by the skipper of the boat *Bin Rouge* who in a magazine article (*Blue Water Sailing*, Sept. 1999) stated: "We sailed into Bass Strait on a forecast of "45-55 knots (of wind), six to eight meters (of seas). I know now, but didn't know then, that this implies gusts to 80 knots and waves to sixty feet. I have seen graphs demonstrating that mean wind strength did not exceed 55 knots, and wave height did not average more than 8 meters (25 feet) at a measurement point outside the countercurrent area. The forecast was strictly correct, but a warning of maximum wind strength and wave height might have made me and about 30 other skippers turn around." (Note: *Bin Rouge* did prudently abandon the race.)

It appears that many race participants (and maybe even a large share of the entire world's boating community) were unfamiliar with the spectrum of wave heights that encompass a single-valued wave height report in a forecast. The single-valued wave height reported in a weather forecast is the "significant wave height" and is the average of the highest 1/3rd of the waves (see earlier table). Figure 8 illustrates over a range of wind speeds that the average height of the highest 10 percent of the waves can be 29 percent higher than the significant wave height which is what forecasters report. To top that off, many boats in the Sydney-Hobart Race faced the one-in-a-thousand wave which was 87 percent higher than the reported significant wave height. It has also been stated that there is a one-in-300,000 wave whose height is four times the significant wave height. Those Sydney-Hobart Race participants who took the forecast literally, were to find out they were not sufficiently schooled in weather forecasting techniques.

To this orderly spectrum of wave heights we can add rogue waves which defy analysis but present themselves as solitary giant waves in random areas of the oceans (also called freak or pyramidal waves). In September 1980 in a typhoon 500 miles south of Japan the 965-foot long bulk carrier *Derbyshire* carrying iron ore from Canada encountered a rogue wave 115 feet high which is said to have been the cause of its sinking.

There is a rhythm in wave trains which statistical analysis indicates that every 7th wave will be the highest. While this may be true in the ideal world, the real world knows that it is possible for two waves of significant height to be in succession followed by a long period of only average height waves. This is also true for shoaling water waves, a fact well-known to surfers who sometimes wait long periods for the best riding wave to appear. It is important to the skipper who seeks to tack his boat or to turn it around in a seaway in order to run with the wind, that he study the wave pattern and make his move when a series of average height or lower waves appear. The period of minimum height waves will not last long so an expeditious move is required.

BREAKING WAVES

As cycloidal waves become steeper, due to either an increasing wind, a wind opposing current situation, or a shoaling bottom, the crests become sharper. The maximum theoretical sharpness of a crest before breaking is about 30 deg to the horizontal as illustrated in Figure 9(a). As the wind further increases and the wave grows taller, the crest will fall over because the simple circular orbiting motion of water particles cannot keep up with the increase in the speed of the surface particles. The wave will then break in a very forceful manner.

Two types of break become possible: the sliding break and the curling break. The sliding break of Figure 9(b) is typical of the confusion of waves in the open ocean where the depth is great. The overfall can be very turbulent and forceful. The curling break of Figure 9(c) is more typical of shoaling water and is the delight of surfers who seek to ride the "pipeline." The power of water in the curl can be awesome, reaching 7000 lbs per square foot force for a 40 foot high wave—approximately Beaufort number 11. After a curler wave breaks, it will degenerate into the sliding type of break. Note that a wave break does not have continuity along the crest, but occurs in sections (see photograph). This allows the crafty skipper to sail between crests thereby avoiding the worst of breaking seas.

The speed of the breaking crest, Δs_b in Figure 9(d), is the speed of advance of the wave itself. This can be visualized as the transfer of the orbital momentum of the non-breaking wave of equal speed into linear momentum at the crest of the breaking wave. The magnitude of the breaking speed for the case of a Force 11 wind wave in deep water is tabulated in Table 2.

Van Dorn offers the following rules of thumb for the frequency of

Duration of blow T (hours)	Wave length L (feet) in deep water	Wave height (h) (feet)	Speed of break Δs_b (knots)
1 ½	100	9	13
4	200	19	18
8	300	30	23
11 ½	400	38	27

Table 2. **Approximate characteristics of breaking waves for 60-knot winds (Force 11).**

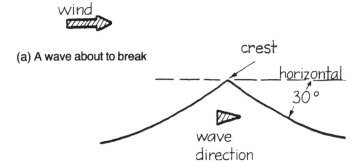

(a) A wave about to break

(b) A wave in the process of breaking as a slider

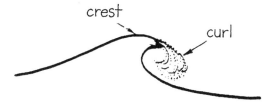

(c) A wave in the process of breaking as a curler

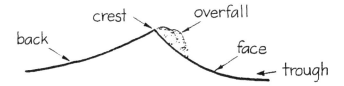

(d) Speed of a breaking crest

Figure 9. Characteristics of breaking waves

Under the right circumstances a breaking wave can be a beautiful work of Nature. Courtesy *Latitude 38.*

breaking waves: for wind speeds under 10 knots, less than 1 percent of the waves break; for wind speeds over 60 knots, 100 percent of the waves break. Between these two extremes there is a linear variation of breaking probability.

The power unleashed by a breaking wave should not be underestimated, nor should it be cause for panic. The shape of the wave is more important than the strength of the wind creating it and its shape deteriorates rapidly from the theoretical sinusoidal shape to plain chaos. When waves begin to break, it is time to weigh the capabilities of the crew and the boat to continue the present passage or to take other survival action.

You should not delude yourself into thinking that the ocean surface is always made up of well-defined and well-behaved wave patterns. It is not. At low wind speeds, you may be able to identify wave height, length, and period, but as the wind increases in strength, wave confusion grows until it becomes the maelstrom of hurricane-driven waves. The reason for this pattern of confusion is that the wind is not steady in direction and each wind direction creates its own waves. When waves from more than one direction intersect, a mixed pattern of waves ensues yielding pyramidal breakers of extreme height.

Add to the wind waves the swells arriving from afar and you have chaotic wave patterns that defy description. When multiple trains of breaking waves intersect, it creates a scene of total confusion, one that is most difficult, if not impossible, to navigate in small vessels. Such was the case in both the 1979 Fastnet Race disaster off the British Isles and the 1994 Queen's Birthday Storm off New Zealand.

While the Coast Guard must press on with its mission in heavy weather, small boats can elect to ride out the storm in relative comfort using modern drag devices. Courtesy U.S. Coast Guard

WIND OPPOSING CURRENT

Finally, it is important to recognize the unreal seas that develop when the wind blows against the current as in the Agulhas current off southeast Africa, the Gulf Stream off the North America east coast and the Portland Race off the coast of Britain. The opposing current causes a compression of the waves reducing their wave length, making them steeper, and causing increased breaking. An opposing current whose speed is 1/10th that of the wind speed can cause the wave height to be increased by 21 percent. An opposing current that is 1/4th that of the wind speed can increase wave height by 300 percent. When the wind blows in the direction of the current, the waves lose much of their steepness and increase their wave length. A following current with a speed 1/4th that of the wind can reduce the height of the waves by about 25 percent.

The impact of wind opposing wave was clearly shown in the 1998 Sydney-Hobart race where southerly and southwesterly storm winds of 45 to 55 knots blew against the 3-4 knots south flowing East Australian Current. Crews afterwards reported the waves in the following manner: "ugly, big and wet"; "treacherous—due to extremely large waves breaking frequently"; "It looked like the 'gates of hell' and building the greatest bitch of a sea you could ever design"; "large breaking waves threatened to overwhelm the boat—they would stand up on the quarter—sometimes dropping on us. ..." Just about every negative aspect of wave generation appeared in this storm.

CHAPTER THREE

Sea Anchor Design

Sea anchors are large drag-producing devices that are deployed over the bow of the boat to hold the bow into the wind and minimize the backward movement of the boat. It is necessary that the anchor be a relatively large device in order to "anchor" the boat to the surface water which is obviously fluid and yielding. (Whereas a drogue is intended to only slow a boat down in its normal forward motion, a sea anchor is expected to essentially hold it from moving on the sea's surface.) A very large parachute-type sea anchor can do this task, but since the water itself is in motion due to wind-driven currents, the boat will still move over the bottom at the speed of the local current.

A boat riding to a large sea anchor has a motion very similar to that of a boat riding to a ground anchor. The biggest difference is in the nature of the wave forms themselves. At sea the waves tend to be longer and not as steep as waves in shoaling waters, but they will still crest frequently. The powerful but irregular motion of the sea when resisted by a sea anchor can produce great strains on the sea anchor gear. The dynamic loading will give all of the problems found in ground anchoring such as overloading cleats and Samson posts, causing severe chafe on the rode, and occasionally burying the bow in green water. The one mitigating factor of the sea anchor streamed from the bow is that it keeps the bow pointed into the wind which is the normal riding position for the boat.

Cruising literature abounds with instances of monohull boats riding out severe storms by lying a-hull and letting the boat seek its own comfortable riding position with respect to wind and wave. This apparently is no longer true since the modern boat design, with its center of underwater lateral resistance well aft and a great deal of lateral windage forward, tends not to weathercock into the wind. Instead, it takes up a beam-on position, life below decks becomes untenable, and the boat is liable to capsize if hit by a breaking wave.

Multihull sailors were the first to make a concerted effort to improve the safety of their craft through the use of sea anchors. They adapted military surplus parachutes as sea anchors with significant success. Randy Thomas writes in *Yachting* (November 1985) of his Pacific circumnavigation:

> On the afternoon of July 25, 1985, *Celerity* sailed out of the fog in Juan de Fuca Strait and secured to the same Victoria wharf from which she had departed on her Pacific cruise eight years before. To complete her Pacific circumnavigation, the 31 foot trimaran became the first multihull to make the non-stop high latitude crossing from Japan to mainland North America.
>
> Hard on the wind for 17 days, *Celerity* also encountered 800 miles of calms and rode out four gales on her parachute sea anchor. She logged approximately 4500 miles, completing the crossing in 48 days without the use of auxiliary power.

There is nothing in boat design that prevents powerboats or sailing monohulls from also using sea anchors when the need arises. A properly sized sea anchor is essentially a parking brake and as such can be used in a variety of situations. Powerboats of all descriptions can use them to hold their bows into the wind and minimize drift while they repair propulsion machinery so that they can get underway again. The difference in working on a cranky engine in a boat when it is held bow to the wind, as opposed to freely drifting sideways, can be the difference between getting the engine back in operation quickly or succumbing to mal de mer. Powerboats experiencing a loss of power near a leeward shore can be in a most difficult situation.

While a sea anchor will not cut the boat's drift to zero, it can provide the skipper with additional time to solve his problem. Certainly any single-engine powerboat would benefit in an emergency by having a sea anchor aboard. Commercial fishermen use them often to hold their boats near the fishing grounds during the night while they sleep.

A sea anchor bringing the bow of the boat into the wind will make a more pleasant ride whether fishing, sunning, sleeping, or doing maintenance. The applicability of sea anchors to work and recreational boats has been widely tested in recent years and their seeming ability to save boats

The airman's parachute adapted for anchoring at sea. Note the many shrouds and the small vent at the crown of the canopy. This 24-foot diameter sea anchor stows in less than 1 cubic foot of space. Courtesy Para-Tech Engineering Co.

under adverse situations is a powerful incentive for more development on all fronts.

Most of the condemnation of sea anchors mentioned in boating litera-ture comes from three correctable causes: (1) too small a sea anchor; (2) lack of a riding sail; and (3) chafing through of the rode. A sea anchor must be large enough to prevent the bow of the boat from being driven off to leeward by wind and wave; a riding sail can help prevent the boat from yawing; and the rode must be protected from chafing. A sea anchor must be viewed as a system and all elements of the system must be in place and in working order for the system to function.

Some writers have said that they want a sea anchor with "give" to it— they don't want to be held firmly against the impact of a wave. The idea that a properly sized sea anchor will "give" with the waves is patently untrue. The large mass of water in a sea anchor* cannot be accelerated rapidly enough to absorb a wave's impact on the hull. A small sea anchor only lets the boat drift to leeward faster and to yaw into a broaching position. As the sea anchor becomes smaller and smaller, the boat begins reacting more and more like a boat that is lying a-hull.

Did you ever think that a larger ground anchor would transmit increased loads to your boat? Certainly not, all it does is assure that you have a more positive grip on the seabed. Similarly, a larger sea anchor gets a better "bite" on the water and is in a better position to withstand the constant loads of the wind and the waves on the boat. The strains on the rode and the hull will be no greater than with a smaller sea anchor that is not slipping. In fact, a small sea anchor that lets the boat yaw excessively will cause a greater strain on the boat when a wave hits it broadside at its greater angle of yaw.

What, then, is different about using a large sea anchor in place of a ground anchor? First, most ground anchoring takes place in the lee of some land, or at least where there is a reef or breakwater to moderate the wave action. Waves, and not wind, are the major factor in either type of anchoring. Where a boat is ground anchored without the benefit of shelter from the seas proportionate to hull size, the waves will be steeper and higher than in the open ocean because of the shoaling waters. That is why boats seek anchorages sheltered from the seas with only secondary regard for shelter from the wind.

In the open sea there is no relief from the waves but they have a longer period and tend to break less frequently than shoal water waves. Sea anchoring with adequate sea room has to be a less worrisome problem than ground anchoring with the shoreline only tens of feet away.

PARACHUTE SEA ANCHORS

In essence, all sea anchors look something like an airman's parachute when in use and, in fact, some are parachutes. A sea anchor has also been referred to as a hydraulic parachute. The independent variable of the sea anchor is its size and, hence, its drag. The dependent variable is its strength

---

* The mass of water in a 9-foot-diameter hemispherically-shaped container is approximately 190 cubic feet, or 12,000 pounds of sea water.

and there is no question that a sea anchor system has to be strong and durable. Worse than having no sea anchor at all is having one that fails in the midst of a storm, allowing the boat to broach and present its vulnerable beam to the onslaught of breaking waves.

The first true sea anchors were airmen's parachutes. (I do not consider the Voss or Fenger types of drogues to be sea anchors, regardless of what their inventors called them.) By itself the parachute is a drag device meant to slow the descent of a stricken aviator to some moderate speed that will enable a safe earth impact. The same parachute when deployed in water develops a drag 800 times as high due to the greater density of sea water. That drag is sufficiently large to counteract the wind loads on most recreational size vessels. Whereas an airman's parachute under the force of gravity allows a descent speed anywhere from 15 to 20 feet per second, the same parachute operating in water will slow the vessel's drift to 1 or 2 knots.

The airman's parachute adapted as a sea anchor does away with the body harness and risers but retains the shrouds and canopy intact. The typical parachute canopy is made of rip-stop nylon (much like spinnaker material) and is made in many gores to give it an approximate hemispherical shape when inflated. Shroud lines and gores are sewn together with the shroud lines passing completely over the top to give the necessary strength. An 18-inch-diameter vent hole is left in the top of the canopy to let some air escape and give stability to the parachute. Reinforcing patches (these may be made of Kevlar) are strategically located at points of load concentration.

Parachutes now used as sea anchors are all of the hemispherical type. Recently, highly maneuverable rectangular parachutes have come on the scene, but their use as sea anchors has yet to be tested. The standard hemispherical airman's parachute when new costs upwards of $1,000, but used and surplus parachutes can be purchased for as low as $50. The saving is most attractive and the parachutes may be still in good shape. Parachutes professionally converted to sea anchors by knowledgeable companies retail for $150 to $200 (plus rode assembly costs.).

Useful rules of thumb have been developed over the years for the proper size airman's parachute to use as a sea anchor. The basic airman's parachute comes in a range of sizes—20, 24, 26, 28, 30, 32, and 34-foot diameters. All of these, however, may not be available at the surplus store at any one time. Larger parachutes have been made for cargo drops from airplanes such as the common 35-foot-diameter cargo parachute. Van Dorn (1974) describes the use of a 100-foot-diameter parachute as a "drogue" [sic] on a weapons test barge.

Two events reported by Para-Anchors International occurred in 1984 that are worthy of note. They supplied a J/30 sailboat with a 9-foot para-anchor* and, in an ensuing storm, the para-anchor pulled the J/30's bow into 20-foot seas and kept it there for 4 hours during which time the crew members were able to rest.

In the other instance a 76-foot steel ketch of 36 tons displacement with a full keel rode to a 28-foot parachute sea anchor for 18 hours in a gale off the Azores. Winds were 55 knots and seas to 20 feet. The skipper reported that "the para-anchor worked perfectly, we rode nicely. I will never make an ocean passage without one on board." (*Force 10 Imminent*, August 1985)

SEA ANCHOR SIZES

The proper size sea anchor for your boat is one that limits leeward drift to less than-knot, preferably 1/2-knot and keeps the bow of the boat headed into the wind. When choosing a sea anchor, err on the side of too large rather than too small. As the sea anchor size is diminished, the boat reacts adversely as though it is lying a-hull and can readily fall into a broaching situation. If the sternward movement of the boat is too fast, as with an undersized sea anchor, the rudder will be put in peril. Modern boats, both sail and power, with a great deal of windage forward ride better if a riding sail is used to hold the stern downwind.

The United States Sailing Association (ORC *Special Regulations* 1996-97) recommends as a general rule that the diameter of the parachute sea anchor should be large enough to: (a) maintain stable inflation without being tumbled by surface action; (b) overcome the lateral resistance of any

---

* The awkward term 'parachute sea anchor' was conveniently shortened to "para-anchor" about 1964 by Patrick Royce, author of *Royce's Sailing Illustrated* (1993). After he had engaged in five months of intensive testing of the parachute sea anchoring concept he determined to his satisfaction that it was ready for use on power and sailboats and coined the shorter name.

keels involved; (c) hold the bow(s) into the seas and keep side-to-side yaw to a minimum; and (d) reduce drift so as to protect the rudder and its fittings.

Although there are some valid analytical techniques available to estimate sea anchor size (see Appendix A and Shewmon, 1998), it is really the actual experience of many users who have provided contemporary rules of thumb for selecting parachute anchor sizes. Since parachute canopies can and are designed to different shapes, a standard measurement system has been invoked which is applicable to all sea anchors. The standard chosen is the one used for airmen's parachutes, after all, the airman's parachutes did come first. The airman's parachute standard of measurement is based on the *uninflated* (flat) diameter of the canopy where the canopies are assembled flat to begin with (as with the Para-Tech Engineering sea anchors). The canopy's diameter, when filled out by water pressure, becomes approximately 70-percent of its *uninflated or flat diameter*. A sculpted-design canopy (such as the Shewmon hybrid hemispherical canopy) is measured only by its *inflated* diameter to which it was initially designed and built. The performance of a sculpted design canopy can be compared to a flat design canopy whose diameter is 1.4 times as great, both having approximately the same diameter when inflated. When comparing performance characteristics of sea anchors using the two different construction techniques, it is important to use only *inflated* diameters for the size reference which is representative of the performance potential of the canopies when in use.

PARA-TECH SEA ANCHOR SIZES FOR MONOHULLS

Para-Tech Engineering Co. is one of the oldest drag device makers in the business today. It has not only made drag devices for boating but parachutes for airmen and a variety of fabric products for both air and water use. Para-Tech sea anchors are made from high strength nylon fabric having a weight and strength of more than four times that of surplus parachutes which have been used for sea anchors for many years. Seams are reinforced with nylon webbing. The design is such that if the full system is overstressed, the canopy will blow a panel before anything else fails. It will still hold the boat but with an increased drift rate.

Para-Tech's original business was furnishing personnel parachutes as sea anchors to the San Diego fishing fleet. The parachutes so used lasted

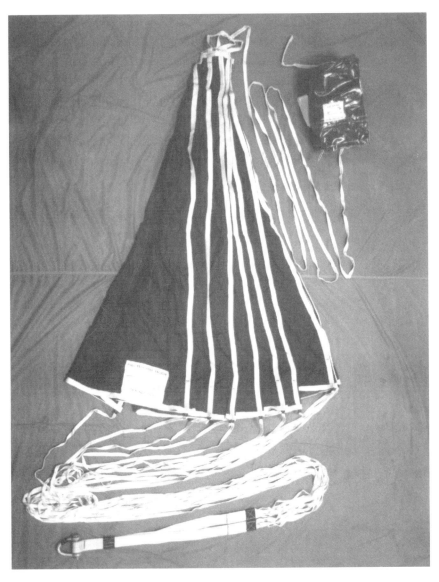

The Para-Tech sea anchor ready for stuffing into its Deployable Stowage Bag (upper right). Courtesy Para-Tech Engineering Co.

in service only one year. In contrast, in 1996, a designed-for-the-purpose Para-Tech sea anchor was returned to the factory worn out after five years of use. The skipper reported that it had spent the equivalent of one year in the water!

In spite of the fact that boats and seas come in almost endless combi-

nations, the growing experiences of parachute sea anchor users have provided enough basic data to produce an empirical size selection technique
based on the length and displacement of the vessel. The following Para-
Tech Engineering Company recommendations are based on years of experience with their product and are applicable to the general run of parachute
sea anchors on the market. Note that the <u>uninflated</u> diameter is used as their
reference measurement. To repeat an earlier caveat, in choosing a sea anchor size, err on the side of too large rather than too small.

Boat length LOA - feet	under 20	under 25	25 to 30	30 to 40	35 to 50	35 to 50	50 to 90	50 to 90	70 to 90
Displacement 1,000 lb.	up to 5	up to 9	up to 12	12 to 25	25 to 35	35 to 45	45 to 65	65 to 95	95 to 150
Sea anchor diameter - feet	6	9	12	15	18	18	24	24	32
Rode material	12-plait braid 6-6 nylon								
Rode diameter inches	3/8	3/8 or 1/2	1/2	5/8	5/8 or 3/4	3/4	3/4	7/8	1

- Data courtesy of Para-Tech Engineering
- <u>Uniflated</u> canopy diameters
- Sizes based upon fin keel sailboats or planing powerboats - full keel
  sailboats and displacement powerboats should use one size larger.

Table 3. **Para-Tech sea anchor size selection.**

SEA ANCHOR SIZES FOR MULTIHULLS

It was John and Joan Casanova who developed the first rule of thumb
for the size of a parachute to use as sea anchor on a multihull boat. They
determined that the diameter must be equal to or surpass the boat's beam

(Casanova et al. 1982). Their 39-foot LOA x 22-foot beam trimaran, *Tortuga Too,* used a 28-foot-diameter parachute sea anchor as standard equipment and survived 80-knot winds off New Zealand and 40-foot seas in the Indian Ocean. They related that the weather was so bad in the Indian Ocean that they spent one out of every six days lying to their 28-foot-diameter parachute sea anchor.

The US Sailing *Offshore Multihull Requirements* presents a general guideline for multihull sailing craft that calls for the diameter of the parachute sea anchor to be at least 35-percent of the LOA. These guidelines apply to both the Para-Tech and Shewmon designs.

Experience has shown that multihull boats lie to a sea anchor better than do monohull boats. This is most likely due to the wide-based bridle attached to the out-riding hulls. The narrow bow of the monohull precludes as effective a bridle spread as in the multihulls, but, nevertheless, ground anchoring experience has shown that even a narrow bridle spread on monohulls reduces the amount of yawing that takes place.

SHEWMON SEA ANCHORS

The Shewmon Company of Safety Harbor, Florida, manufactures a line of sea anchors fabricated for the specific purpose of sea anchoring. They are designed to insure self-opening and to produce maximum pull at minimum drift speeds. The canopy of a Shewmon sea anchor is made from 7 1/4-ounce polyester cloth heavily reinforced at critical stress points. Canopy ropes are stitched into the canopy panel joints with polyester thread, providing excellent carry-through strength from the panels to the shroud lines.

The strength, performance, and stability of the Shewmon sea anchors have been verified by the manufacturer's own testing program in which developmental and production sea anchors have been towed behind powerful harbor tugs at speeds up to 8 + knots. Besides confirming the strength and drag of the sea anchors, the tests have proven their stablity in operation.

In a comprehensive technical report (Shewmon 1998) the manufacturer gives an analytical method for estimating wind drag forces on a boat and water drag counter-forces, which combine to set the pull of the sea anchor. Two numerical examples of drifting speeds are given for boats bow to windward:

The 10-foot-diameter Shewmon Mark III sea anchor was designed for use with ships as large as destroyers and has a strength of 60,000 pounds. The latest Mark-9 design has been made as large as 27 feet in diameter. Courtesy Shewmon, Inc.

36-foot sloop in 60 knot winds	.94 knots with a 5-foot sea anchor
	.72 knots with a 6-foot sea anchor
	and a steady state pull of 680 pounds
48-foot motor yacht in 60-knot winds:	1.7 knots with a 5-foot sea anchor
	1.4 knots with a 6-foot sea anchor
	and a steady state pull of 1,600 pounds

The above examples would indicate that a 5-foot sea anchor is suitable for 36-foot sloop in the winds considered, but the 48-foot motor yacht probably should have at least a 7-foot sea anchor to ensure that motion astern is never large enough to cause rudder damage.

SEA ANCHOR PERFORMANCE

The common shape of sea anchors is a truncated hemisphere, which provides an efficient drag shape with no requirements for stiffeners and which, if properly designed, will open automatically when deployed.

The 4-foot-diameter Shewmon Mark III sea anchor. Courtesy Shewmon, Inc.

Shewmon, Inc., has done extensive testing on such sea anchors and has developed drag data for a variety of sizes and drift speeds ("Calculating Sea Anchor Performance" by Daniel Shewmon, *Cruising World*, June 1984, and "Survival with Sea Anchors" by Daniel Shewmon, *Cruising World*, March 1984). Dan Shewmon has kindly consented to allow the reproduction of some these data in my own format, as shown in Figure 10.

Although there are no theoretical limits to the maximum value of the allowable drift speed, the practical limitation is how much backward loading a rudder can withstand before failure. I would suggest that the upper drift speed limit never exceed 2 knots. For overall design purposes I would suggest using a 1-knot drift speed.

Parachute-type drag devices are quite suitable as sea anchors where the speed through the water is low, say below a couple of knots. When higher speeds are encountered (as in drogue applications), the parachute-type drag device becomes directionally unstable, tending to move sideways and even to develop large amplitude lateral oscillations. This axial instability makes them generally unsuitable for drogue applications even in very small sizes.

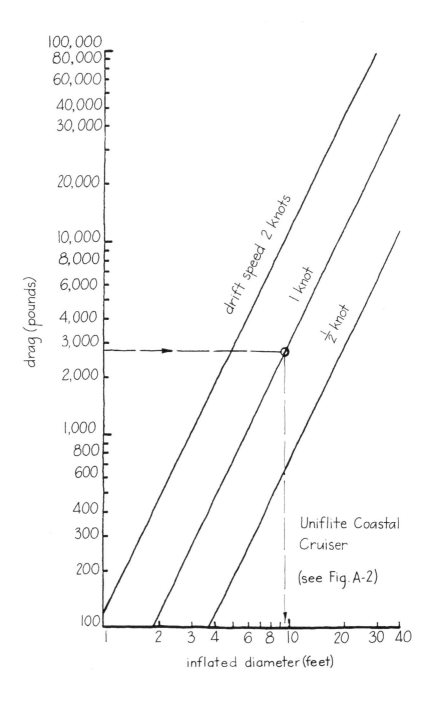

Figure 10. Sea anchor drag. By permission of Shewmon, Inc., ©1983.

MAKING YOUR OWN SEA ANCHOR

Making your own sea anchor is not impossible, but the results may be less than desired unless an extensive testing program is carried out before the sea anchor must actually be deployed in heavy weather. Three critical factors must be considered: size, stability, and strength. You can estimate the size and load for a sea anchor by one of the means described in Appendix A.

Canopy materials should be heavy synthetic cloth; polyester or nylon are preferred candidates because of their all-around durability. Material weight should be between 3 and 5 ounces and the sewing should conform to the best sailmaking standards. Puckers and gathers should be meticulously avoided. Opening shocks of a poorly deployed sea anchor and surge loadings could split poor seams, weakening the canopy assembly.

When you design the rope connections for the sea anchor, make allowances for the following strength reductions:

Bowline	60% of rope strength
Anchor bend over a 5/8-inch-diameter ring	75% "
Eye splice with thimble	90-95 % "

Webbing, too, suffers a marked reduction in strength due to being folded and having stitching penetrating its body. Parachute makers' tests have shown that folded and sewn webbing has an assembled strength of only 70 percent of the virgin webbing. Allow for this in your design.

Stability of the canopy under load depends mostly on the ratio of shroud length to <u>uninflated</u> canopy diameter. As an absolute minimum the ratio should never be less than one. Shorter shrouds result in smaller inflated diameters. A shroud length of over 2 <u>uninflated</u> canopy diameters appears unnecessary from a canopy opening standpoint since longer shrouds do not allow the canopy to open any farther. Instead, they tend to cause an instability in the sea anchor. Long shrouds promote canopy rotation, resulting in a shortening of the shrouds and entanglement of the trip line if one is used. There is also a greater tendency for the sea anchor to oscillate in the water when longer shrouds are employed. A shroud length ratio of 1.25 to 1.5 times the <u>uninflated</u> canopy opening diameter is a good place to start with your design.

There is really no proven way to test your homemade sea anchor's performance short of heavy weather use. Shewmon's sophisticated testing system using 1,500-horsepower harbor tugs is well beyond the resources of the person who feels it economically expeditious to make his own sea anchor. The only alternative is for the skipper to take his boat out in the heaviest weather deemed safe for a test and actually deploy the sea anchor without an emergency being the driving force behind the deployment. The sea anchor can then be observed for adequate drag (at that wind speed), stability, strength (at that wind speed), and general behavior in deployment and retrieval. Such an experience will pay off later when the sea anchor must be deployed under more trying conditions.

Small weights are sewn to the hem of the Shewmon sea anchor to prevent rotation. Courtesy Shewmon, Inc.

JURY-RIGGED SAIL SEA ANCHORS

In an emergency sailboats can make use of a sail as an improvised sea anchor. Low aspect ratio sails work the best, but any will do in a pinch. Simply attach shroud lines to tack, clew and head, making them of such length that they simulate equal length shrouds of an equivalent circular sea anchor as shown in Figure 11. Gather the shrouds together and connect them to a rode and your sea anchor is ready to go. Do not be concerned about having too large a sea anchor due to the size of the sail at hand. A large sail will put no more strain on the boat than a smaller one. Remember the ground anchor analogy.

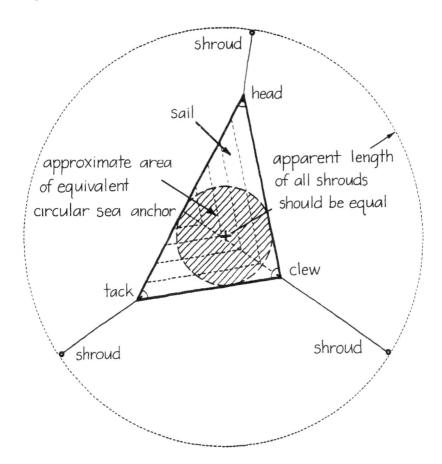

Figure 11. Using a sail as a sea anchor.

Shewmon points out that the improvised sail sea anchor is not as efficient as the built-for-the-purpose circular sea anchor. If you have used a gaff-rigged sail, then the efficiency is about 70 percent. For a triangular sail, it is about 50 percent. Also, a sea anchor made out of a sail will tend to be unstable and will yaw back and forth as the water spills alternately from one edge or the other, but it will furnish drag and that is what you are after in an emergency.

There is no simple way to trip a sail sea anchor, so you will have to move the boat up to it when the emergency is over, either using the motor or by winching in on the rode. The sail should be thoroughly washed afterwards with fresh water (the next rain?) before being dried and stowed away. Check it for damage at the clew, tack, and head fitting and repair as necessary. Now you have time on your side.

CHAPTER FOUR

Sea Anchor Use

The components that make up a sea anchor system are similar to those of a ground anchor system except for the anchor itself:

Ground anchor system	*Sea anchor system*
deck gear	deck gear
rode	rode
ground anchor	sea anchor
trip line (in some cases)	trip line (in some cases)

You generally use the same deck gear for a sea anchor as you use for a ground anchor. The reason is obvious—it is there and it is sized for the job of "anchoring." The ground anchor rode can be used as part of the sea anchor rode although a dedicated sea anchor rode is preferred. The design of a sea anchor rode is critical to its success. A sea anchor rode of improper length, inadequate strength, wrong construction, or incompatible components can doom the vessel it was intended to aid.

RIGGING THE SEA ANCHOR

The components of a fully rigged sea anchor for a monohull boat are illustrated in Figure 12. The monohull sea anchor rode is brought aboard the boat in the same manner as a ground anchor rode—through a well-faired bow roller with plenty of chafing gear. Only one swivel is possible in the monohull rode and that is placed at the apex of the shroud lines of the sea anchor.

A sea anchor swivel should be of quality stainless steel of an adequate size. Its purpose is to allow the para-anchor to "free-wheel" and allow the rode to detorque itself. The swivel should be inspected before sea anchor deployment to be certain that it is free to do its job with a minimum

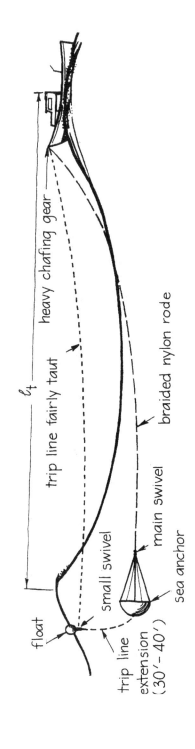

Figure 12. Rigging the sea anchor for a monohull vessel.

of friction. Shewmon does not believe that swivels will, indeed, swivel freely enough so he does not recommend them. Instead, he adds lead weights to one side on the parachute canopy to keep it oriented by gravity at all times. (See previous photograph.)

A trip line can be attached to the apex of the sea anchor to help in the eventual retrieval of it. The trip line and the trip line extension can be made of 3/8-inch diameter nylon braid or plaited rope. A floating trip line would be preferred but polypropylene rope tends to kink and tangle too easily to be used for this purpose. One of the newer synthetic ropes that have good strength and elastic properties and floats as well may be the best answer although their cost is a bit high. The trip line must be longer than the deployed rode to be certain that it does not accidentally trip the canopy in surging seas. Partial trip lines can also be used and they reduce the possibility of tangling the trip line with the rode resulting in the inadvertent tripping of the canopy.

The sea anchor float can be any docking fender, but one of the spherical, fluorescent floats is the best for visibility. When the sea anchor is deployed, it is this float that tells you how far upwind your sea anchor is, allowing you to position it one wave length (or multiple thereof) upwind of your boat. A small swivel is also used where the trip line and trip line extension connect to the float eye. The length of the trip line extension should be 1 1/2 to 2 times the height of the largest wave to allow the sea anchor to work below the depth of the main orbital motion of the wave particles.

The fabrication of the rode assembly should follow the best practices of putting together a ground anchor rode: tight eye splices around proper thimbles which are seized in place, safety-wired shackles, freely moving swivels, chafe protection where needed, and great care to prevent tangling of lines in stowage.

During use, chafe prevention should be your number one worry. Generous size cleats (a Samson post or bitt is preferred), large radii fairleads, and leather or corded hose chafing gear must be used. All the while the sea anchor is deployed, its attachment to the boat must be inspected frequently and, if chafe is developing, a fresh nip must be taken on the line.

The most severe chafe on the rode will probably take place where the rode passes over the bow roller or chock. This can be alleviated through the use of a length of chain attached to the braided nylon rode.

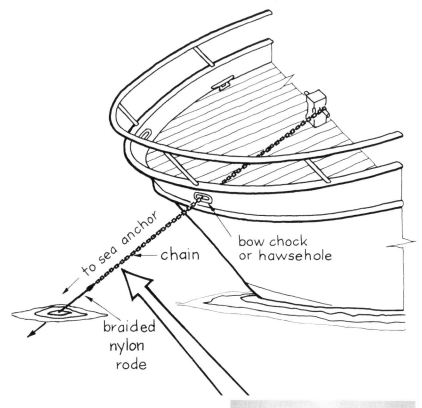

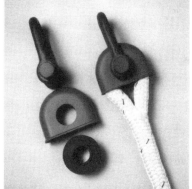

The Samson Nylite connector is a 3-part assembly: a spool, a shield, and a special shackle. It can be used with either braided or twisted synthetic rope. This is a major advance in the technology of linking rope to chain. Courtesy Samson Ocean Systems, Inc.

Figure 13. Eliminating chafe at the bow roller. The illustration shows a recommended way to connect a chain to a rope rode to prevent chafing of the rope where it passes through bow rollers or chocks designed to handle the ground anchor rode.

The attachment should be made with a non-chafing connector such as the Samson Nylite connector (Figure 13) or other thimbles for storm anchor rodes shown in my book on anchoring and mooring (Hinz 1999). This solution implies that the rope part of the rode will be a fixed length and that any length adjustment be made by letting out additional chain. A good starting length for the braided nylon rode would be about 200 feet with the option of adding up to 100 feet of chain. There is a limit to the amount of chain that can be added since the weight of the chain will tend to sink the sea anchor too far.

Multihull sea anchor rodes must be brought symmetrically to the hulls through the use of a bridle, as illustrated in Figure 14. The key to the use of a bridle is to have the included angle less than 30° in order to minimize the lateral loading put on the hulls. Bridle lines should be run through snatch blocks and then back to cleats so that the symmetry of the bridle as well as the overall length of the combined rode-bridle can be adjusted as the wave length of the sea changes. It is common practice to make the diameter of the bridle lines equal to that of the rode although one size smaller is adequately strong.

The bridle on a multihull provides a benefit not found on the single tether of the monohull and that is it holds the multihull directly into the wind better, minimizing the amount of yawing that takes place. The bridle swivel isolates any rotation of the rode from the bridle lines.

RODE LENGTH

Many (if not most) references relate the rode length (ℓ_t) to some multiple of the boat's length, say 10 boat lengths, or to some arbitrary length such as 200 feet. Neither is correct, although there may be an occasional set of waves where each length becomes appropriate by chance. Rather than resorting to chance, however, one can use a clear rationale to determine rode length. This is based on the wave length of the sea for the particular seaway at hand.

Consider the relation between adjacent wave crests, the sea anchor, and the boat as shown in Figure 15. When both sea anchor and boat are riding on crests (or in troughs) as in Figure 15(a), they experience the same orbital motions of the surface water and, hence, move in harmony with each other. There is no added acceleration loading due to differential speeds.

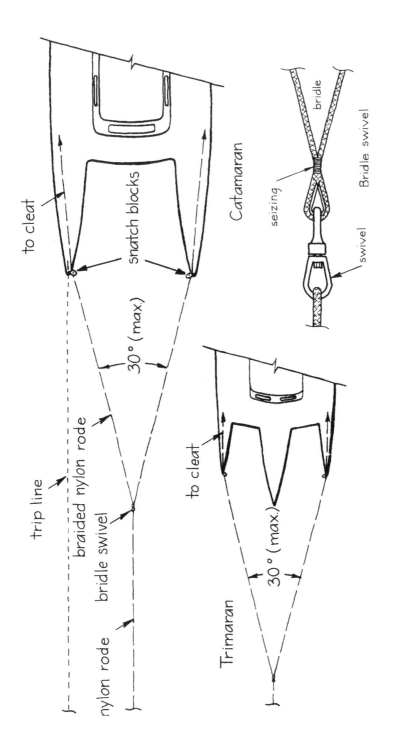

Figure 14. Rigging the sea anchor for multihull vessels.

In this case the rode length (ℓ_t) is nominally equal to the wave length L.

If the rode length is less than the wave length, then the boat may ride a crest while the sea anchor is in a trough as shown in Figure 15(b). Relative to the boat then, the sea anchor will be accelerated forward while the boat will be accelerated aft. The result in all probability will be a torn sea anchor body, a failed rode, or the rode attachment on the boat being torn asunder. Whatever happens, the boat will then be left to broach, roll, or pitchpole, none of which is an attractive alternative to providing a suitable rode length in the first place.

If the boat is riding a trough while the sea anchor is riding a crest as illustrated in Figure 15(c), then the rode will experience a complete slackening with the possibility of the sea anchor being caught up in the wave overfall. This could lead to the shroud lines becoming entangled and the sea anchor not reopening. The consequences of that happening need not be stated.

It is essential that the length of the sea anchor rode be matched to the wave length of the sea (or a multiple thereof) for a particular wind condition. What, then, should the actual length of the rode be?

Figure 16 has been developed to give the practical rode length for various winds as measured by Beaufort number and for various durations of blowing of those winds. An unlimited fetch has been assumed. According to *Bowditch*, the actual wave length of a sea is about two-third's that calculated by Equation 1 and this has been plotted in the figure as the rode length. Note that the rode length varies with both the duration of the blow and the intensity of the blow, hence the need for an adjustable rode.

Determining the proper length of a sea anchor rode in seas raised by a steady state wind is fairly easy using the foregoing method, but when it comes to seas raised by shifting winds, the solution is not so clear. Confused and disorderly seas are the norm for gales that approach from a direction different than the prevailing wind. In this case it would be hard to identify the critical wave length by Figure 16. Under these conditions, then, you must resort to an "eyeball" length determination. Assuming that you have a highly visible fluorescent docking fender as a float, adjust the rode length to match the wave length of the dominant wave form.

A point should also be made regarding the length of the rode to be used in a shallow body of water, such as the Great Lakes. The same prin-

wind

(a) $\ell_t \approx L$ (correct)

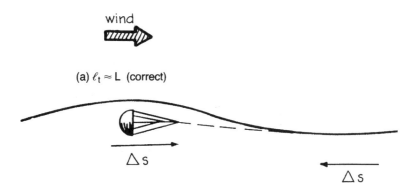

$\triangle$ s

$\triangle$ s

(b) $\ell_t < L$ (extra heavy load)

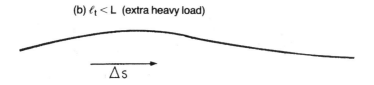

$\triangle$ s

(c) $\ell_t < L$ (ineffective)

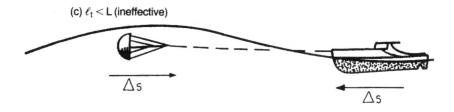

$\triangle$ s

$\triangle$ s

Figure 15. Matching rode length to wave length.

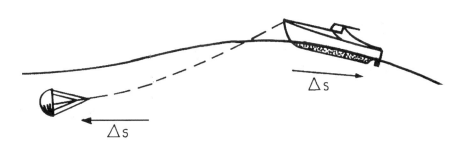

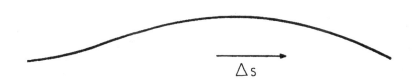

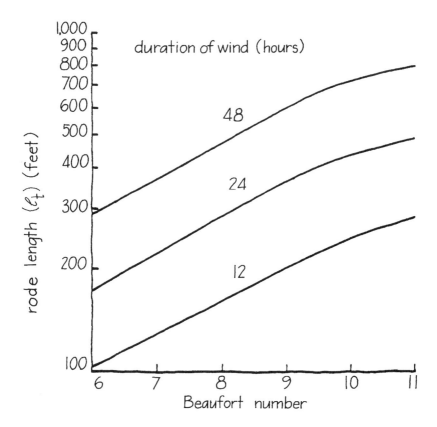

Figure 16. Length of sea anchor rode.

ciples should be followed; that is, the rode length should be an integral wave length long. But, because one wave length in shallow water may be quite short, some of the benefit of elasticity of a long rode is lost, so consideration should be given to making the rode multiple wave lengths long, thereby preserving the elasticity while still matching wave lengths to minimize jerking.

When the rode of a parachute sea anchor goes slack, the sea anchor simply relaxes and floats in the water looking much like a jellyfish since there is no speed differential with the water. It will have no tendency to tumble or turn itself inside out unless it operates too shallow and gets caught in the overfall. In general, a length of chain in the rode helps to keep it below the wave's significant orbital motion depth.

The problem of providing length adjustment to the rode while also assuring chafe protection is a knotty one but amenable to a solution. Chain is the best anti-chafing gear and can be used in an adjustable length rode. Based on Figure 16, my choice of the basic rode length would be 300 feet. This accommodates low Beaufort number storms of significant duration and the beginnings of stronger storms. The rode would be fitted with a length of High Test chain to ride over the bow roller as in Figure 13, but it would be only a short length. Then, another length of nylon rode, say 100 feet, would be connected to it followed by another short length of chain. Two more lengths of nylon interspersed with two more short lengths of High Test chain would be attached to yield a total of 600+ feet of rode, mostly rope. This rode is adjustable in 100 foot increments to approximate the wave lengths of the apparent largest waves. In the confused seas of storms, it will be difficult to quantify rode length closer than 100 feet allowing good anti-chafe protection at acceptable increments of rode length.

RODE STRENGTH

The desired strength of the rode is not amenable to a simple mathematical solution. There are simply too many unknowns in the equation. As seen in Figure 17, we have at least five drag components to consider, of which only one, the wind drag, is anywhere near definable in a rational manner. The drag due to crest overfall is highly dependent on the intensity of the wave break. The drag due to the boat's tendency to backslide down the face of the wave depends on what pitch angle the boat assumes at any instant in time. The inertial drag of the boat depends on the relative orbital speeds of the sea anchor and the boat, as well as the elasticity in the rode and the ability of the boat to accelerate forward with the sea anchor.

To untie this Gordian knot, we must resort to practical experience, which also helps us with the logistics of our sea anchor gear. Most instances of sea anchor deployment have seen the use of the ground anchor rode as the sea anchor rode. This may have been an expedient in those cases, but it has worked successfully and it is available. Maybe the rode need not be of such size, but to make it smaller runs the risk of promoting failure, within the limited knowledge that we have. Until some boat fits a load-measuring system in a sea anchor rode and goes out in stormy seas, we had better stick with what practical experience has told us.

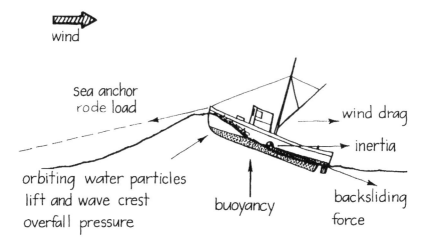

Figure 17. Forces on a boat riding to a sea anchor.

You can estimate the size of the rope anchor rode for your boat by one of the two methods described in my book on anchoring and mooring (Hinz 1999). The length of a rode may need to be considerably longer than a ground anchor rode (meaning that your boat must carry extra line on board of the proper size and there must be a means of connecting lengths together in a reliable manner). Such a scheme is suitable for the coastal sailor who will try to avoid stormy seas whenever possible. For the blue water passagemaker, however, it would be prudent to carry on board a made-for-the-purpose sea anchor rode.

The rode, just like a ground anchor rode, must have elasticity to absorb surge loads. For this reason nylon rope is the best choice. But the type of construction is not so clear. One of the characteristics of a sea anchor is to rotate if it has a chance. When 3-strand rope construction is used, there is every opportunity for it to rotate even though swivels are used in the rode. A rotating sea anchor can entangle the trip line and render the canopy ineffective. To avoid this, braided (or plaited) nylon rope may be preferred even though there is some loss of elasticity. This provides the non-rotating feature as well as some elasticity to cushion wave impacts on the boat. The strength comparison of these two forms of rope construction is shown in Table 4 . Braided nylon is 25-35 percent stronger than twisted construction with a higher allowable working load. Its elasticity, however, is only 60 percent that of twisted construction, as seen in Figure 18. For this reason, if you substitute braid for twist, match them on the basis of breaking strength and not diameter. That way you retain maximum elasticity in a rode of smaller diameter.

Diameter of rope		3-strand twisted nylon		Braided nylon	
inches	millimeters*	Breaking strength (pounds)	Recommended working load† (pounds)	Breaking strength (pounds)	Recommended working load‡ (pounds)
3⁄8	9	3,700	410	4,800	960
7⁄16	10	5,00	550	6,500	1,300
1⁄2	12	6,400	700	8,300	1,660
9⁄16	14	8,000	880	11,200	2,240
5⁄8	16	10,240	1,140	14,500	2,900
3⁄4	18	14,200	1,560	18,000	3,600
7⁄8	22	20,000	2,200	26,500	5,300
1	24	25,000	2,750	31,300	6,260

Table 4. **Strength of ropes (dry).**

*Closest metric rope size.
†Working load is 11% of average breaking strength.
‡Working load is 20% of average breaking strength.

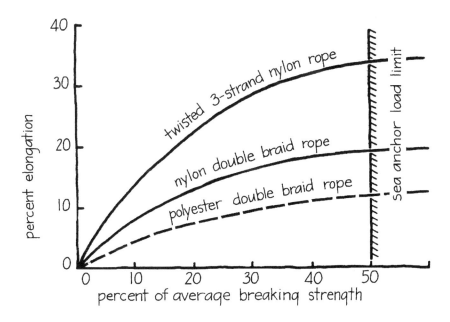

Figure 18. Elongation characteristics of synthetic rope.

Kenneth Bitting conducted a test program for the US Coast Guard on the dynamic behavior of double braid and 8-strand plaited nylon and polyester ropes as used in ship mooring applications (Bitting 1980). His work confirmed that the elasticity of synthetic ropes is highly dependent on the rate of load application. Some of his results:

- Dynamic elasticity of nylon and polyester ropes may be only 25 to 30 percent of the static elasticity when instantaneously loaded.
- Dynamic elasticity of nylon and polyester ropes is markedly decreased after exposure to years of saltwater immersion.
- Nylon and polyester ropes lose up to 50 percent of their tensile strength after 4 to 5 years of saltwater immersion.
- Nylon rope can withstand higher dynamic loading if some tension is always kept on the line.

What we do not know is the rate of onset of dynamic loads applied by the sea anchor (or drogue) in order to quantitatively assess the loss of elasticity in a rode. Since boats using sea anchors have never reported a rode failure due to jerking (abrasion doesn't count), we have to assume for the present that the rate of load application is less than used in Bitting's work and the rope's full elasticity is available.

Writers have commented on holding the boat too firmly. One says, "A possible danger in using a sea anchor is that the boat might be tethered or held too firmly against the seas so that she cannot yield" and "Even if the modern boat can be made to lie reasonably well to a sea anchor forward and a riding sail aft, there are certain disadvantages in this method, a major one being that the boat will at times be thrown backwards, and this could very possibly damage the rudder."

The question of holding the boat too firmly is answered by the elasticity of the rope which, as in ground anchoring, allows the rope to stretch to relieve the surging load. That is much better than having a too-small sea anchor which allows the boat to drift aft at such speed (or acceleration) that the rudder is put in jeopardy or the boat falls beam-to the waves.

As for the boat being thrown backwards, that is not likely to happen if the proper length of rode is used such that both boat and sea anchor ride in fields of orbiting water particles traveling in the same direction This is critical and the bulk supply of rope carried on board should be long enough to permit lengthening the rode should the wave length further increase with an increase in the wind.

DEPLOYMENT

You are probably wondering by now how to deploy the sea anchor. There is only one answer to that—with great care. If you are deploying in a storm, you will have strong winds and seas to contend with and getting any part of your sea anchor hung up on the boat's rigging or fittings can be disastrous.

If your sea anchor is fitted with a trip line and float, they should be laid out on deck in the order in which they will be deployed; float, canopy, trip line and rode in parallel, and then the bridle, if one is used. Ascertain that all shackles are safety-wired and that the bitter ends of the rode and the trip line are attached to the proper deck fittings. The entire assembly should be able to lift off the deck (over the pulpit/lifelines!) without catching on any of the boat's gear or tripping the crew.

Deployment of the parachute sea anchor takes place off the windward side of the drifting boat or, if downwind control can be maintained, the sea anchor can be deployed over the stern, but the rode is still attached to the bow. The general procedures recommended by the Para-Tech Engineering Company are as follows:

1. Head the boat into the wind, allow the sails to luff and the boat to stall. Secure the rudder amidships.
2. Wearing a safety harness, deposit the sea anchor in its Deployable Stowage Bag along with trip line, float line and float into the water on the windward side of the boat (never on the leeward side where the boat may drift over it and foul the lines and chute.)
3. Allow the boat to drift away from the parachute, paying out the rode off the deck slowly and snubbing up on it occasionally to help the parachute to open and rotate the bow of the boat into the wind.
4. Continue drifting away from the parachute until the required length of rode is deployed. Keep some tension on the rode to prevent the parachute from initially sinking too deep.
5. When the proper length of rode is deployed (boat and parachute are riding in the same parts of the waves), make fast the line and install

the necessary chafing gear. Adjust length of trip line as necessary.

6. Retract centerboard(s), daggerboard(s), swing keel, etc. Furl mainsail and/or mizzen sail(s) in a seamanlike manner and take a coffee break.

Be aware that when the canopy fills, the remaining rode and the trip line on the deck may pull away fast, so be certain there is nothing to snag the lines in their haste to go over the side. When the rope reaches its bitter end (which you have secured to a strong fitting, haven't you?), the boat will turn quickly into the wind and assume the bow-on riding position. Should any deployment foul-up occur, secure the trip line short until it can be cleared. Then give the canopy its freedom again and finish the deployment.

A story ran in *Yachting* magazine (May 1987) that indicates some of the trouble that you may experience in deploying a sea anchor. The 76-foot Palmer-Johnson motorsailer *Scheherezade* had departed New England in December 1986 on a passage to Bermuda when it ran into some of the Atlantic's worst weather. The story reads:

> With 30 to 40 foot seas, thunder, lightning, heavy rain and hurricane force winds blowing, it was almost impossible to distinguish the ocean from the heavens. At 0200 the winds suddenly dropped from 70 to 30 knots, then to zero—the eye of the storm, apparently. Our hopes brightened until a couple of hours later, when the winds picked up again to 50, 60, then 75 knots. Suddenly the stainless-steel staysail halyard broke, and the staysail blew out. With no engine, no sail, no speed, the boat began drifting sideways. The large roller-furling jibs were unusable in this kind of weather, and there was no spare staysail halyard. We put out a parachute sea anchor, but its 300 foot, one-inch nylon line got fouled in, or around, the propeller/rudder and obviously got severed by the knives meant for cutting fishing lines loose.

(The *Scheherzade* eventually was returned to a New England port under Coast Guard tow.)

Riding to a sea anchor, the boat will have two mechanical problems to overcome. One is with the rudder and the other is with the propeller. While riding to the sea anchor, the boat will very slowly move astern and it will also occasionally fall astern as the rode alternately snubs up and loosens as waves pass under it. To protect the rudder, it should be firmly lashed amidships before the anchor is deployed. If the boat has a tiller, the tiller must be firmly secured in place. If the boat has a wheel, the problem becomes more difficult to solve, since locking the wheel may still leave a lot of spring in the cable system. In this case, the rudder should be provided with a hole at the trailing edge through which a securing line to each quarter can be attached. It is critical that the rudder be fixed in place to prevent it taking up a side load if the boat is thrown backwards. Self-steering systems should be similarly locked in place or lifted from the water to avoid damage.

The propeller problem is one that is unique to folding propellers. As the boat surges fore and aft, the blades of the propeller will alternately open and close. It is unlikely that this motion would permanently damage the blades, but it will make objectionable noises in the boat (which are unneeded when tensions may be running high enough already).

Many monohulls will not ride steadily bow-on to the wind; instead, they will tend to sail off on one tack or another. This results in severe lateral loads being applied to the stem fitting where the sea anchor rode comes aboard. If the stem fitting is actually on a bowsprit, then the side loading may exceed the sprit's strength. To counter this problem, your sea anchor rode can be rigged with a "Pardey bridle" which is simple and effective. The bridle shown in Figure 19 was developed by Lin and Larry Pardey while sailing their 24-foot LOD (length over deck) *Seraffyn* around the world (*Sail*, August 1982). It is essentially a barber haul applied through a snatch block to the sea anchor rode. The barber haul is belayed to a cockpit winch while the rode is belayed forward to a substantial cleat or Samson post. The angle at which the boat rides to the sea anchor and the wind can be adjusted to yield the best ride under the immediate conditions. As with ground tackle, chafe must be prevented at cleats and a fresh nip should be occasionally taken on the pendant to keep the line fresh.

Another trick to counter tacking back and forth while riding to a sea anchor is to fly a "riding sail," a trick often used when ground anchored for the same reason. A single surface sail, as in the mizzen of a ketch, does not work very well because of the dead spot when the apparent wind angle goes to zero causing the sail to tack. Flogging of the sail occurs at this point which is hard on the nerves and even harder on the sail. A better scheme is to make a wedge-shaped riding sail as shown in Figure 20 which will al-

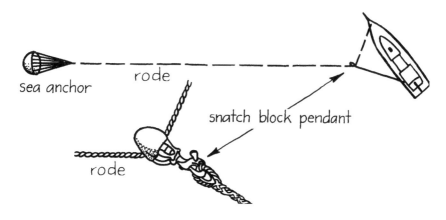

Figure 19. Pardey bridle.

ways have some lateral force when the wind tends to tack it. Further, there
is no shuddering of the sail when it changes tacks. This sail is custom made
for each boat and can be fitted to both sloops and ketches, the ketch being
relatively easy. One nice thing about the wedge riding sail is that it works
equally well for ground anchoring.

NAVIGATION

Navigation with the sea anchor deployed will be mostly a matter of
tracking the current and estimating the downwind drift of the boat due to
the small slippage of the sea anchor. Both current and downwind slippage
are about the same magnitude. In the open sea there is little to worry about,
but around islands, coral, or other landmasses, a continuous GPS or DR
plot should be kept to foreshadow any problems. Should your track plot
show that the boat is going to drift onto land, there are two choices depending on what is known about the land characteristics. If it is a gradually
sloping, good holding bottom, and the winds are not too strong, it may be
possible to deploy your ground anchor to snub up while still offshore. If the
shoreline is rocky, fast shoaling, and very deep, you had best retrieve the
sea anchor while you have time and get the devil out of there. A boat not
under control near land is certain to have a precarious future.

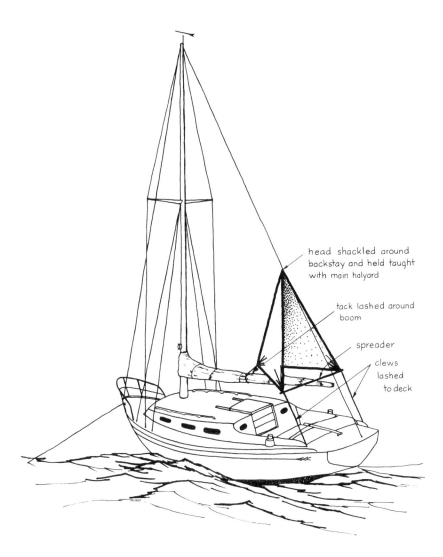

head shackled around
backstay and held taught
with main halyard

tack lashed around
boom

spreader

clews
lashed
to deck

Figure 20. Using a riding sail.

RETRIEVAL

Sea anchor retrieval would be very straightforward if it were not for the elements that forced you to deploy it in the first place—strong winds and high seas. If the winds and seas are down, retrieval can be easy, but if you are descending on a lee shore and need to retrieve your sea anchor during the storm, it can be difficult.

To retrieve a parachute sea anchor, haul in on the trip line, dumping the canopy. To do this you most likely will have to put the trip line on a winch or windlass because the initial loads may be quite high (and that is the reason for having a 3/8-inch trip line). Beware a springy nylon trip line, though, that is brought in at near-breaking strength of the line. If the line is taut and it should break while in the air, it will have a nasty snap back to the boat. If the line is immersed in the water when it breaks, in all probability the snap back will be totally damped by water friction. This would be a good reason to have a line with minimum elasticity as your trip line, e.g., a braided polyester line reserved for the purpose.

A somewhat easier way to retrieve a sea anchor equipped with a trip line is to snub up on the trip line and then carefully ease out on the rode, allowing the trip line to upset the canopy as the rode goes slack. The collapsed sea anchor is then hauled in with the trip line.

A third method of retrieval can be used with any sea anchor whether or not equipped with a trip line. It is the obvious winching of the boat up to the sea anchor using the anchor windlass or some other winch-like device on board. When the main swivel has been brought on deck, grasp a shroud line or two and pull it aboard, dumping the canopy. The one problem with this technique can be found in the loads on the canopy due to the heavy weight of water in it. It may be necessary to hitch an auxiliary line to the chosen shrouds until the canopy spills its water contents. Conversely, the auxiliary line can be simply attached to a strong cleat and the rode eased out until it goes slack as in the preceding method. Then the sea anchor assembly can be handed on board.

Needless to say, in any deployment or retrieval of a sea anchor, great care should be exercised. Crew members should be wearing safety harnesses and be well instructed in their duties. All lines should be free to run outside of the boat, and not entangled with each other or other parts of the boat. Should a tangle occur during deployment, retrieve the sea anchor, clear the impediment, and then redeploy more carefully. Do not become complacent about the possible loads on a sea anchor—they are high and they are dynamic!

CARE OF THE SEA ANCHOR

Inspection requirements for the sea anchor (or drogue) system fall

The 53 meter fishing boat *Daniel Solander* hanging off a 33 meter diameter Coppins sea anchor in 11 meter waves off the coast of New Zealand. The rode is seen leading directly forward into the wave. Courtesy W.A. Coppins Ltd.

into two categories—those associated with the rode and those associated with the canopy. In the case of the rode assembly (including bridle and trip line, if used), take the following actions as soon as possible after the winds and seas have subsided:

1. Rinse out the synthetic lines with fresh water and dry them thoroughly. Do not allow sea anchors or drogues and their rodes to dry out after being wetted with sea water. The resulting salt crystalline growth will cut the fibers. Sunlight should also be avoided on the nylon elements.

2. Inspect lines for chafing or hockles (twisted construction rope). If any severe chafing exists or hockles have appeared in the twisted construction lines, replace the lines. Consign the old rope to making up dock lines or other less critical applications.

3. Examine twisted construction lines internally for broken or frayed fibers that appear to be fused together due to excessive heat generated

by high loading (as, for instance, around cleats or a Samson post).

4. Check thimbled eye splices in the lines for looseness or rusting of thimbles. Rust can be damaging to rope.

5. Clean each shackle or swivel in the rode and apply graphite grease to swivel. Be certain that swivels are free to swivel. Safety-wire all screw pins.

Inspection of the canopy assembly should cover the shroud lines, the canopy proper, and the trip line attachment, if any. Perform the following steps after each use. These can be accomplished on the vessel's deck in calm seas and light winds. The latter is quite important in the case of an airman's parachute sea anchor.

1. Rinse the canopy and shroud lines with fresh water and dry thoroughly.

2. Check each shroud from main swivel to canopy looking for abrasion damage. Check loop at swivel for secure fastening and examine stitching of line to canopy for looseness or breaks. If knots are used at either end of shroud, be certain that they are tight and that the free end is lightly stitched to the main rope to prevent loosening of the knot.

3. To check the canopy, start at the apex of one gore and inspect the gore material and radial seams from end to end looking for tears, snags, and loose stitching. Continue the same process until all gores have been inspected. Pay particular attention to the shroud line attachments.

4. Check the strength of the fabric by firmly pushing a finger into it; do not use the fingernail, especially on parachute canopies, as it could penetrate the fabric of a perfectly good canopy. Aged nylon, particularly that which has been exposed to the sun for long periods, should be carefully examined.

The sea anchor assembly can be packed after it has been rinsed, dried, inspected, and repaired (if necessary). The canopy is folded first, the shroud lines next, and, finally, the rode assembly. To fold the canopy, stretch it out along the deck, securing the apex to a cleat. Pick up each shroud line in turn and accordion pleat each gore until all gores have been folded and lie on top of each other. Do this when the winds are light. Then roll the canopy up, starting from the apex and continuing to the midpoint. Secure this bundle so that it can't unroll and then proceed to prepare the shroud lines. (Refer to photograph on page 41 for a folded sea anchor canopy and shrouds.)

Stretch the shroud lines out on deck and comb them with the fingers to remove kinks and overlaps. Be certain that the lines have not been inadvertently turned inside out; if they have, turn them back so that no line overlaps any other. Gather the lines together and snake them back and forth on the unrolled portion of the canopy starting at the canopy skirt attachment. Allow the main swivel to hang out one side and then roll the canopy and lines together starting at the skirt end and rolling towards the center to meet the previously rolled part. The completely rolled canopy can now be put into a bag for storage with the main swivel on top. The sea anchor bag should be stored in a dry location on the boat where it is protected from sunlight, spillage of any liquids, or possibility of mechanical damage.

The sea anchor rode after inspection and repair, if necessary, should be carefully coiled up like any valuable line on a boat, and hung up in a ventilated locker or sail bin where it is readily available and will not get tangled. When the sea anchor rode is also used as the anchor rode, maintain it as described in my anchoring book (Hinz 1999) so that it remains a trustworthy line.

RULES OF THE ROAD

The *"International Regulations for Preventing Collisions at Sea - 1972"* apply to all vessels upon the high seas making no differentiation between vessels which are commercial, naval or recreational or if involved in inclement weather or not. Rule 2(a) clearly states "Nothing in these Rules shall exonerate any vessel, or the owner, master or crew thereof, from the consequences of any neglect to comply with these Rules or of the neglect of any precaution which may be required by the ordinary practice of seamen, or by the special circumstances of the case." While it is hardly likely that a recreational vessel having a collision with a ship would cause enough damage to the ship for the owner to pursue court action against the recreational vessel, it is conceivable that the ship could collide with the recreational vessel when lying to a sea anchor and the vessel's owner would want to take action against the ship's owner. There is also the slight possibility that two recreational vessel's could collide in a storm with the need to assign legal responsibility to one or the other parties.

The proper rules of the road to be followed when lying to a sea anchor are not specifically identified in the "Rules of the Road." This is not surprising since the probability of vessels meeting when one or both are under sea anchor constraints is extremely small. Although sea anchors go back in history to the 17th century, they were never popularly used until the 20th century and then only by recreational vessels. It is hardly likely that this will change as those who make the rules are primarily concerned with ships of commerce and navies. The welfare of small craft on the high seas are of secondary interest and such vessels are expected to comply with rules as issued by the international bodies.

The first question that arises is whether a vessel lying to a sea anchor is underway or not. Rule 3 (i) states: "The word 'underway' means that a vessel is not at anchor, or made fast to the shore, or aground." Therefore, a vessel lying to a sea anchor would be considered to be underway and must display a proper combination of masthead, sidelights and stern light according to Rules 23 (power-driven vessels underway) or 25 (sailing vessels underway). The display of an anchor light or black ball (Rule 30) would violate this rule and impart false knowledge that the water is shoal enough for ground anchoring.

The question of being underway but not making way through the water clouds the issue a bit. A vessel lying to a sea anchor makes only minimal way through the water although it may be making noticeable movement over the ground because of ocean currents. The Rules, however, do not take into account movement over the ground as being separate from movement through the water. If, indeed, the vessel at sea anchor is not making way through the water and it is not rigged to do so, it possibly could be termed a vessel not under command, falling then under Rule 3 (f) as being "unable to keep out of the way of another vessel." If that is the case, it would carry the two all-around red lights in a vertical line as prescribed in Rule 27 (a) for vessels not under command and not the masthead, sidelights and stern light for being underway. Such lights and shapes for a vessel not under command are not usually mounted on a recreational boat and it is doubtful whether any recreational boat owner would put them on his boat. The foregoing interpretation would also seem relevant to a boat that is lying a-hull sans sails.

Should the vessel be carrying a sail in addition to a sea anchor (as in the Pardey bridle configuration), then it probably would be considered to have some degree of maneuverability definitely requiring the lights of a vessel underway. A sailboat which is hove-to under sail alone would certainly be considered to be underway and should carry the appropriate navigation lights.

In the instance of a power-driven vessel whose primary propulsive power is not operative by reason of mechanical failure (not just shut down for convenience) and is lying to a sea anchor, could seemingly be designated as a vessel not under command.

Regardless of what arguments you bring forth regarding appropriate lights and shapes for a vessel lying to a sea anchor, one rule overrides all the rest and that is Rule 5, Lookout. A continuous lookout by sight, hearing and radar (if so equipped) is required at all times. It is not enough to just show what you believe to be the proper lights, you must also continuously appraise the situation around your vessel and assess the possibility of a collision happening. Be prepared to contact any closing vessel by radio or with a bright light flashing the code letter "D" meaning "Keep clear of me – I am maneuvering with difficulty." It would also make sense to fly the Code Flag D when lying to a sea anchor and claiming to be underway. Since a masthead strobe light is not specifically forbidden in the rules for International waters, setting one flashing at the masthead when the possibility of collision appears imminent would seem reasonable, but a masthead anchor light would not.

While nobody looks forward to having to defend themselves in an Admiralty Court following a collision at sea, your chances of winning are greatly improved if your vessel was displaying the proper lights or shapes and had a lookout posted at the time of a collision. If it was not, then the burden of proof is laid upon you to prove that you did not violate the rules and, therefore, could not have contributed to the collision. If you have violated the rules in a collision incident, then you are deemed to be at fault and probably will not be able to collect damages. It has been observed by many that Admiralty Laws are far more convoluted than civil or criminal laws and are to be avoided by judiciously following the published Rules of the Road even in heavy weather when the stress of survival is uppermost in your mind.

CHAPTER FIVE

Specialty Sea Anchors

Author's note: In speaking of drag devices for special applications as with life rafts and other safety gear, the distinction between what is a sea anchor and what is a drogue becomes confused because such safety gear does not usually have a definable bow nor stern. To simplify matters we will in this chapter refer to drag devices for special applications simply as sea anchors having tethers.

LIFE RAFT SEA ANCHORS

All life rafts are equipped with an attached sea anchor. Coast Guard-approved life rafts for 4 to 25 persons require a second anchor to be also carried, unattached, in the equipment bag. There are two jobs which the life raft sea anchor must do—one is to minimize drift and the other is to add stability to the raft.

Very few rafts have a capability for sailing under any degree of control and it is best to "anchor" them to the water and minimize the wind drift, accepting as inevitable whatever current drift may occur. This also enhances rescue attempts by minimizing the search area to track current-only movement. A sea anchor capable of holding a raft to current drift speeds is small, indeed, as will be seen later.

The second function of the sea anchor is to provide stability to the life raft in high winds and seas. Several years ago the Cruising Yacht Club of Australia ran a series of tests on life rafts in the open sea and found that conventional rafts without a sea anchor were susceptible to overturning even in moderate seas. Later the British National Maritime Institute, with the cooperation of major British, Danish, and German life raft manufacturers and the Icelandic Directorate of Shipping, conducted extensive open sea tests of life raft stability (40 knots of wind or higher and sea state 9 or higher). They found that the only rafts to capsize were those whose sea anchors failed and the crew was unable to attach another. These tests were so conclusive as to the importance of the sea anchor to stability that design of the ballast bags became of lesser importance than previously thought (*Yachts & Yachting,* 12 March 1982). This is not to say that the concept of the large hemispherical ballast bags or the large toroidal ballast bags are not also viable means to improve the stability of a liferaft, but they, too, require the services of a suitable sea anchor.

Other conclusions reached were that the usual sea anchor made with a square fabric canopy has a strong tendency to tangle in its shrouds and become ineffective, but the conical type on a long tether sinks below the wave action and becomes extremely effective. Life rafts with conical sea anchors used in conjunction with water ballast bags were completely stable in winds to 78 knots. Those rafts without sea anchors would capsize nine out of ten times in 55 knots of wind.

The final sea anchor design recommendation was a conical shape made out of a close mesh polypropylene netting. Later tests indicated this design to be completely successful in preventing raft capsize even when one raft lost all of its ballast bags. Note that a conical-shaped drag device must either have a vent at the apex of the cone or be made of porous material to be stable in drag.

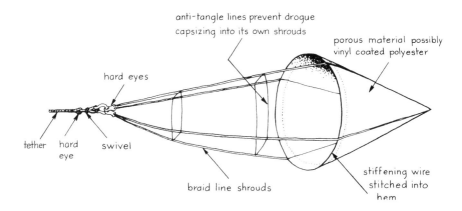

Figure 21. The British National Maritime Institute recommended sea anchor design for life rafts. The porous cone provides stable drag and the shrouds have anti-tangle lines.

The largest life rafts in common use today are 25-man rafts equipped with two sea anchors—one attached and the other in the survival pack. The sea anchor provided with a 25-person life raft is a vented sphero-conical type with a mouth opening of 24-inch diameter, a vent of 3-inch diameter, and a length of 18 inches. Six shroud lines of 45-inch length attach to the canopy at one end and to a 40-foot long, 1/4-inch-diameter, braided nylon tether at the other. The tether in turn attaches to a D-ring on the end of the rectangular raft (see photos).

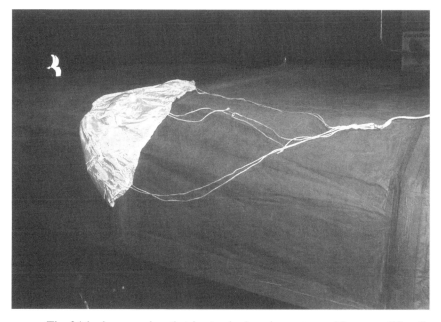

The 24-inch sea anchor that is standard equipment on a 25-person life raft. Photo by the author.

The adequacy of this sea anchor can be estimated by a simple calculation of the drag of the raft and the drift speed with the wind. Using the methods described in Appendix A, a 60-knot wind load on the raft is approximately 150 pounds. The drift speed with the attached sea anchor would be about 1 1/4 knots in the 60-knot wind. The mass of water inside the sea anchor canopy which would have to be accelerated for a wave to overturn the raft is approximately 270 pounds. The 1/4-inch tether has a breaking strength of 1,600 pounds so the sea anchor is capable of resisting a 5- to 6-

G acceleration, thus providing substantial restraint to a wave overturning the life raft.

Scale model tests by Jordan (1984) substantiated the ability of a drogue to stabilize a life raft:

> Preliminary tests were conducted with models of the six man life raft (86-inch diameter full size with a 24-inch diameter disk-type drogue). In the 20-foot simulated breaking wave, the unballasted life raft with no drogue was violently tumbled. In a simulated 8-foot breaking wave, the raft would be capsized about half of the wave strikes. The provision of either a drogue or a hemispherical ballast bag prevented capsize in the 8-foot wave. In the 20-foot wave neither the drogue nor the ballast bag prevented capsize in most cases. However, with the hemispherical ballast bag, the raft would immediately right itself after capsize.

One life raft in the 1979 Fastnet Race carried eight men from the abandoned boat *Trophy*, but it was capsized several times by the wind getting under one edge of the raft and flipping it over. It did not have a working sea anchor. Two of the crew were lost in one of the capsizes. After the fifth capsize, the two flotation rings parted and the crew huddled in the lower ring which had the floor. They finally found the sea anchor, which had been so tightly wound up in its tether that it would not open by itself. The survivors cleared the tether and deployed the sea anchor over the side. It effectively slowed the raft's drift and steadied its motion, but soon afterwards the tether parted. The raft subsequently rolled over several times before the occupants were at last rescued (Rousmaniere 1980).

It becomes patently clear from this tragic episode that both wind and wave can overturn a life raft. It is further evident that care must be taken in deploying the sea anchor and that the tether must be durable enough not to chafe through. A properly deployed sea anchor can materially add to the stability of the life raft in severe seas.

The weak spot in life raft sea anchor design is the tether system. Many life rafts have been overwhelmed by the seas when the tether has broken, not because it was too small in diameter, but because its attachment to the raft and the sea anchor was compromised. While a 1/4-inch braided line tether meets the strength requirements, its attachment to the flotation tubes is critical. On one 25-person Coast Guard-certified life raft, the tether is knotted to a D-ring held on with a rubber patch in tension. This poses two problems: one is that the patch cement is not very strong in tension, and the second is that the single attachment point in the center of the end of the raft would provide little yawing stability to the raft. A preferred attachment would be to lead a bridle to both sides of the raft, securing it to patches which are put in shear, thereby enhancing the yawing stability given by the sea anchor.

But is a 1/4-inch diameter braided tether too small for other reasons? Survivors of the 1998 Sydney-Hobart race complained of the life raft tether being too small in diameter and when they had to manipulate it to clear other lines, it severely cut hands. The Review Committee's recommendation was to increase its diameter but not its strength (CYCA, 1999). It has been the author's experience that any line on a boat under 3/8-inches diameter carrying a load is too small for positive gripping.

Small liferafts (up to eight persons) have a tether of approximately 25 feet in length, however, some are known to be as short as 15 feet. A

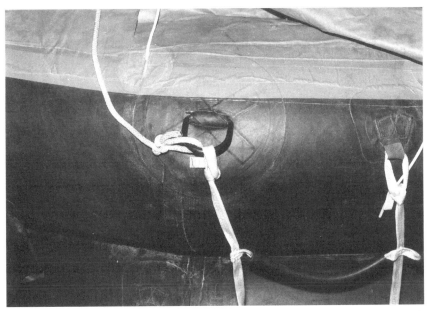

A questionable sea anchor tether on a 25-person life raft. The reasons that it might be unreliable are that the tether is fixed to the D-ring with a knot that can loosen; the D-ring patch is placed in tension when the sea anchor is under load and could fail; and the sea anchor is attached by a single tether instead of a bridle that could stabilize the raft's direction relative to the wind. Photo by the author.

preferred tether length is about 50 feet.

Smaller life rafts, like the 8-person octagonal raft commonly used by cruising boats and small commercial vessels, carry a sea anchor with a 12-inch mouth opening, a 3-inch vent, and a 12-inch long conical body. The drift rate of such a sea anchor-raft combination is about 5 knots in a 60-knot wind.

It is obvious that the small sea anchor on the 8-person life raft is totally inadequate for the raft from a drift speed standpoint alone. The fact that it is a smaller capacity raft than the 25-person model has led manufacturers to assume that a smaller sea anchor can be used. Wrong. The wind drag area of the 8-person raft is about 19 square feet, while the wind drag area of the 25-person raft is 21 square feet—almost the same! In the case of overturning, the 18-foot length and larger passenger weight of the 25-person raft would deter capsizing to a much greater degree than the 7 1/2-foot diameter octagonal raft carrying a maximum of 8 persons. Furthermore, an octagonal (or nearly circular) raft, which loses its sea anchor, is highly susceptible to a phenomenon known as 'carouseling' where the raft rotates rapidly (as a carousel) causing dizziness in the occupants. The rectangular raft is not without its problems on loss of the sea anchor. It almost immediately positions itself broadside to the waves ready to be rolled. (A similar undesirable maneuver in a boat is called a broach).

One can draw a simple conclusion from the foregoing discussion and that is both the 8-person life raft and the 25-person life raft of approximately the same frontal dimensions should have 2 to 3-foot diameter sea anchors. Anything smaller invites capsizing in heavy seas and high winds. Along with the appropriate sea anchor size there is the need for a proper attachment of the tether to the life raft. Only a bridle with fittings attached to the sides of the raft so that the rubber patches are in shear should be used. ("Sides" of an octagonal raft are established when the entry flaps of the raft canopy are to leeward.) Because sea anchors and their tethers take such abuse when in use, a spare sea anchor should always be carried in the survival pack.

The shape of the sea anchor is also of importance since it has been pointed out in the U.K. tests, as well as by Shewmon's tests, that simple square canopy sea anchors do not always open of themselves. A properly designed canopy shape will open even without a rigid ring at the opening.

Airmen's parachutes have been doing it for years! Be certain that the sea anchor used with your life raft has had successful opening tests run on it.

MAN OVERBOARD POLE SEA ANCHORS

Sea anchors in small sizes are now basic parts of survival equipment for blue water sailing. The familiar man overboard pole on racing and cruising sailboats utilizes a baby sea anchor to slow the drift of the signal pole and life buoy in the wind. A typical assembly of man overboard gear is shown in Figure 22, along with the nominal dimensions of the sea anchor for its use. A good baby sea anchor will have a stainless steel wire spring sewn in the hem of the opening to assure instant opening when it hits the water. Without a sea anchor, the emergency gear could well drift faster than the person in the water and soon be out of reach of his swimming ability.

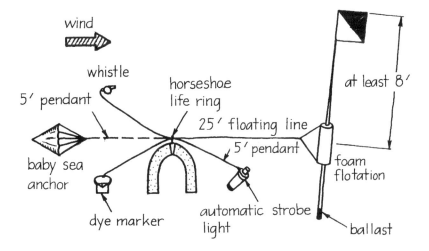

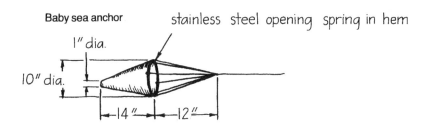

Figure 22. Man overboard gear.

Some horseshoe buoys are fitted with "built-in drogues" to "slow the drift in the water." These are in an embryonic state of development and are inferior to a proper baby sea anchor. The ones I have seen have a visor-type drogue. For the present, the baby sea anchor should be used for man overboard drift control.

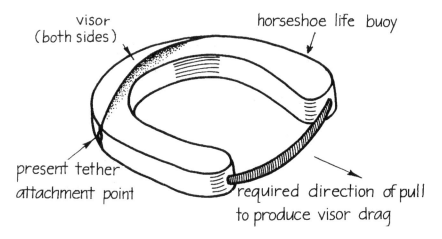

visor
(both sides)

horseshoe life buoy

present tether
attachment point

required direction of pull
to produce visor drag

The horseshoe life buoy with a built-in "sea anchor" is the latest offering in safety equipment for the boater. While the idea has merit, the implementation still needs work. The "visor" sea anchor should have its tether attached at the open end of the horseshoe instead of at the closed end as is now the case. The visor sea anchor is a far less effective drag device than the baby sea anchor of Figure 22.

BOAT BRAKES

Boat Brakes is the name of a patented sea anchor of very novel design that has a place on every fishing boat or powerboat up to 26 feet in length; used in tandem, Boat Brakes can also handle larger boats. Basically, the Boat Brake is a parachute that has a trip line attached centrally to the crown, allowing the crown to be drawn towards the opening and thereby reducing the volume and drag of the device. The control rope (trip line) operates independently but parallel to the tether and is virtually foul proof. A system of weights and floats on the canopy opening prevents the canopy from rotating and tangling shrouds, tether, and control line.

Boat Brakes have a hemispherical canopy made of 2.9-ounce fluores-cent orange urethane-coated rip-stop nylon which is very substantial and durable. The manufacturer recommends the following sizes be used with different boat lengths:

Diameter (feet)	Volume (gallons)	Recommended for
2	42	Trolling in light and medium boats
3	147	Medium fishing boats, bass boats, etc., to 14 feet
4	351	Medium duty boats to 26 feet in length
5	660	Heavy duty boats to 33 feet in length*

*This includes the use of two Boat Brakes in tandem if required.

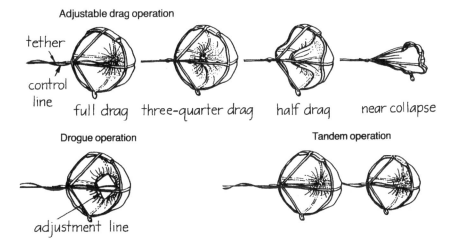

Figure 23. The Boat Brake sea anchor. Courtesy Para-Tech Engineering.

The Boat Brake comes with one unusual feature for a sea anchor and that is the ability to convert it to a drogue. This is done by partially freeing the adjustment rope (which closes the canopy vent when it is in use as a sea anchor). The adjustment rope can be stopped-off with a knot at the desired vent opening to allow the water to flow through the device in a manner similar to a conical drogue. This would certainly have some merit for use on small boats where a single device doing the job of two conserves space and finances.

MENGLER FISHING ANCHOR

From Australia comes a specialty sea anchor designed for deep-sea fishing in windy areas. The Mengler sea anchor is a parachute design that utilizes the umbrella principle for drag control as well as retrieval. It looks like an umbrella when stowed, taking up very little space, and opens like one, forming a parachute canopy for drag.

The secret to the Mengler design is the use of a hollow brass stem to which the canopy shrouds are attached and through which the trip line passes to the float. The length of the trip line between float and canopy crown determines the depth at which the sea anchor will operate. To retrieve the sea anchor, the float is lifted from the water, drawing the crown of the canopy inside to the brass stem and essentially closing the canopy. The unit is then lifted from the water and the canopy is wrapped around the stem for temporary stowage until it can be flushed with fresh water, dried, and then stored until the next fishing trip.

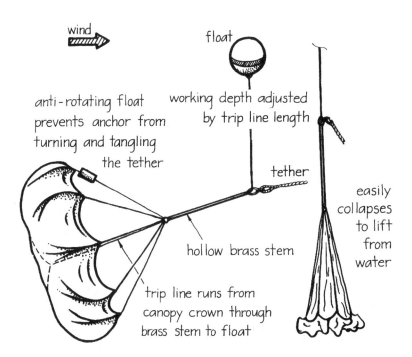

Figure 24. Mengler sea anchor. Courtesy R.D. Mengler.

The Mengler sea anchor has proven itself in Australian waters for deep-sea fishing by slowing the boat's drift away from the fishing hole. While originally designed for boats to 35 feet in length as a drift anchor, Mengler has extended its line to larger sizes, even one for a ship of 200 feet in length. A fishing sea anchor, however, should not be considered a survival sea anchor because it has neither the size nor the durability to withstand storm conditions. The manufacturer recommends the following sizes be used with different boat lengths:

Vessel length - feet	Canopy diameter - feet		Inertial load - tons
	Uninflated size	*Inflated size*	
25	4	3	0.5
35	6	5	1
50	9	7	2.5
75	12	9	5.4

TROLLING SEA ANCHORS

A series of trolling sea anchors with mouth diameters of 18, 24 and 30 inches are marketed by the Cal-June Company under the trade name of Jim Buoy. They are conical in shape, made of yellow vinyl-coated nylon fabric and 1-inch polypropylene webbing shroud lines. They are intended strictly for drift fishing and not for storm use. In a pinch they can be used for steering at low speeds in event of loss of the rudder. Cal-June also makes a US Coast Guard approved sea anchor for commercial ship's lifeboats equivalent to that shown later in Figure 36, including the 1-gallon galvanized steel storm oil container.

THE SEA BUCKET

Do not sell short the usefulness of a sturdy canvas sea bucket aboard your boat. It can perform multiple duties as a bailer, sea water carrier for washing the deck and as an improvised drogue for smaller boats. Hervey

Garrett Smith in his book *The Arts of the Sailor* describes how to make a proper canvas deck bucket with a wooden mast hoop rim which can also do the drogue task at low speeds. Creative Marine Products currently markets a vinyl fabric model with a stainless steel rim which is 11 inches in diameter and can be squashed to 1 inch depth for stowage. As a drogue it develops 65 lb. of drag at 6 knots making it useful for steering small boats which have lost the use of their rudder. Its strength, multi-purpose functions and collapsibility for stowage make these sea buckets useful additions to the boat equipment inventory. Metal and plastic buckets will fail quickly when used for the drogue function and are bulky to stow.

CHAPTER SIX

Drogue Design

One of the better ways to combat high winds and seas while underway is to tow some drag device from the stern of the boat to slow it down and let the waves pass beneath the keel. Unlike using a sea anchor tethered to the bow of the boat, you only want to slow the boat down, not stop it. The philosophy of the drogue is to prevent the boat from surfing down the front of the wave and also to hold the stern down so there is less chance of pitchpoling. Another factor identified years back by the redoubtable Captain Voss is that you do not want the vessel to turn sideways on the crest of the wave, a maneuver called broaching which tends to roll the unfortunate boat over. This is of particular concern when running across channel entrance bars which have waves breaking over them.

The proper speed for a boat being restrained by a drogue is slow enough so that it doesn't surf, but fast enough so that a rolling graybeard does not impact it at full strength. You will also want to maintain good rudder control to assure that the stern is held into the waves even though they may change their approach angle from time to time. Some boats have even been able to steer a moderate course across the waves, making better speed towards their destinations. That, however, must be experimented with so that you don't get the waves too far on the quarter and promote a broach.

So what is a good speed to ride the storm wave? That depends on boat, crew, and wave structure. A racing crew in a boat with a powerful rudder can surf to their heart's content until, possibly, a rogue wave comes along. Cruising boats should probably be held to under 5 knots but not less than 3 knots, the speed at which rudder power becomes seriously diminished. Each boat will behave differently under a drogue and each storm will produce a different set of wave patterns which must be experimented with to find the best (safest) speed.

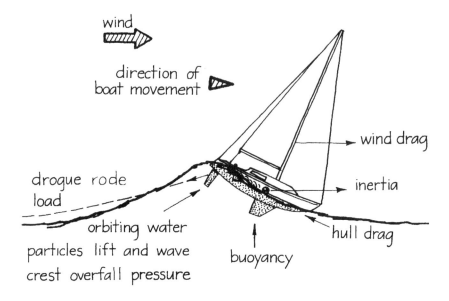

Figure 25. Forces on a boat towing a drogue in heavy seas.

It must be fully understood, when you slow a boat down below the speed of the advancing sea, that an occasional wave can roll aboard, deluging the stern of your boat. You must be prepared with closed cabin hatches and entries and a clean cockpit that you can easily pump out when it becomes a bathtub. While some sailors have negative thoughts of center cockpit designs, they will think again when running before heavy seas.

The design of the stern of the boat will be a major factor in the success of using a drogue under survival conditions. A transom stern shape has the least structural strength while the canoe stern has the greatest potential strength. A transom stern with full bilges will lift easily with the wave while the canoe stern will tend to be buried. A transom stern will take the full impact of the breaking wave while the canoe stern will more smoothly part the crest and let it pass along the sides. Taking the breaking waves slightly on the quarter can materially decrease the impact loads on square transoms.

JURY-RIGGED DROGUES

There are no brakes built into boats to slow them down, so external devices must be used. To date the drag devices employed have been limited only by the imagination of the skippers. Generally they have been jury rigs ranging from automobile tires to ground anchors. The only thing that hasn't been reported being put to use is the galley sink, and I would expect that has been tried aboard some boat later posted missing.

Warps are the most commonly used jury drag devices and their performance is a greatly disputed issue. Robin Knox-Johnston (*Cruising World*, April 1986) described a system he used when transiting the Southern Ocean in *Suhaili*. From the stern of his 10-ton canoe-sterned boat he streamed 600 feet of "2-inch" rope* in a large bight (loop) with a smaller bight of the rope at the center of the larger bight. He related that the bight kept the stern into the waves at all times and removed the danger of rushing down the front of a wave and broaching.

David Lewis encountered a 45-knot gale in *Cardinal Vertue* and attempted to weather it by streaming a 37-meter long (122 feet) rope in a bight astern. As he tried to steer before the wind, the yacht became unmanageable, persistently running across the seas and repeatedly broaching-to. The rope hindered steering and each large sea swept it alongside (Lewis 1961).

The larger 9.5-meter (31-foot) sloop *Samuel Pepys*, when running in a hurricane-force wind in the North Atlantic under bare poles, streamed 73 meters (240 feet) of 28 mm (1 1/8-inch) nylon rope in a bight and two separate 23 mm (7/8-inch) hemp ropes each of 36 meters (120 feet). These drags reduced her speed to 3 knots and cut a smoother track through the seas stern-on, but an attempt to move out of the path of the storm by bringing the wind on the quarter at once resulted in heavy water coming aboard. The seas were estimated to exceed 30 feet in height with a length of 400 feet (Hiscock 1981).

Bernard Moitessier, the indomitable French solo sailor, learned the hard way about losing steering control when towing drag devices. On his way to Cape Horn in the 40-foot double-ended ketch, *Joshua*, he was overtaken by a great gale and ran before it with five trailing warps weighted with seven 40-pound iron pigs. These, he said, had no apparent effect on the yacht's speed and they prevented *Joshua* from correctly answering her helm.

---

*It is believed that the 2 inches referred to is the circumference, a past method of measuring rope sizes. In today's practice it would be a 16 mm or $^5/_8$- inch-diameter rope.

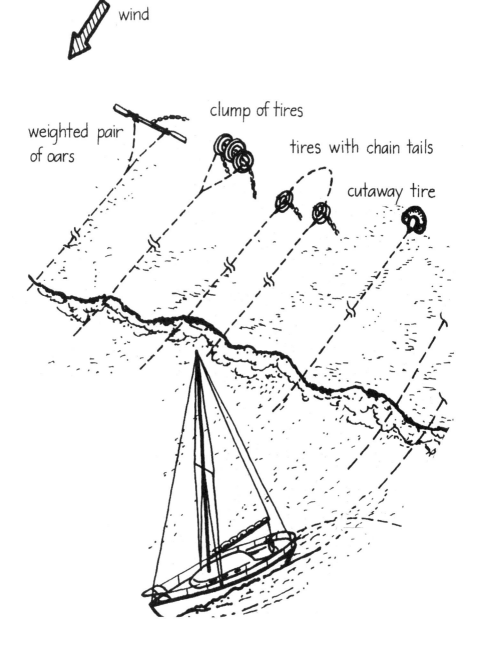

Figure 26. Makeshift drogues.

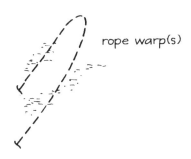

rope warp(s)

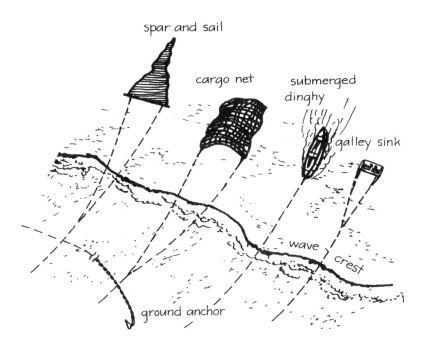

spar and sail

cargo net

submerged
dinghy

galley sink

wave
crest

ground anchor

Since Moitessier didn't like what was happening, he finally cut the drags free and, under bare poles, flew before the gale, steering every inch of the way and taking each crest at an angle as near as he could manage to 15° on the stern.

Joshua's failure to answer her helm was in all probability due to the warps being attached well behind the rudder. But if the warps had enough drag to negate rudder control, then they must also have had enough drag to slow *Joshua* somewhat (Moitessier 1969).

Trailed warps just do not have enough drag to be effective. John Rousmaniere in *Fastnet, Force 10* relates how *Grimalkin*, a 30-foot sloop, was trailing 600 feet of line and "she surfed wildly down the face of the waves, like an elevator cut loose from its cable, and threatened to pitchpole, or somersault over her bow. She once accelerated to over 12 knots and tilting forward until she was almost vertical, plunged down the face of a huge wave." This storm not only produced large waves, but they were steep and confused. *Grimalkin* was later ravaged by capsizes and knockdowns until she had to be abandoned.

It is still fashionable in gamming sessions to discuss the towing of warps and one is led to believe that simply dragging a rope from the stern will do the trick. Shewmon, Inc., streamed 170 feet of new 2 1/4-inch diameter 3-strand polyester rope behind a tug at 10 1/2 knots. Although the rope had considerable tension in it, the pull was actually less than the 300-pound static friction breakout load of the measuring device. Certainly this adds credence to the inability of simple towed warps (especially without a bight) to be dependable in an emergency.

Ross Norgrove (1980) used a wooden "sea anchor" built like a Fenger drogue to slow down his *White Squall* in heavy seas. He said it was the ideal weapon for her when laid over the stern. What he didn't like about it was the trouble of handling such an awkward device.

Eric Hiscock, the dean of cruising sailors, used a "small sea anchor" to reduce the speed of *Wanderer III* from 5 1/2 knots to 1 1/2 knots while running under bare poles. This allowed him to steer across the wind adequately to avoid an island in his downwind path. On another occasion he lay for four days with his "sea anchor" over the stern and the helm unattended, which is a rare success (Hiscock 1956).

Bob Griffith, while circumnavigating Antarctica in his 52-foot

Awhanee, found it best in winds of 80 knots to tow a lot of drags, including the spinnaker boom and several anchors and chains. He kept the seas on the quarter all the time because that helped to reduce speed and rolling. This is similar to Moitessier's experience running without the drag devices (Griffith 1979).

One of the most unusual drag devices to be employed as a drogue was on the 35-foot Piver trimaran *Zulane* on a passage from the Cape of Good Hope to the West Indies. Skipper Frik Potgieter deployed his mizzen boom with the mizzen sail still attached and ran off under bare poles. He stated that the sail had a "calming effect on the seas" (Henderson 1979).

Towing tires has been another technique prescribed for holding the speed of a boat down to manageable proportions. I suppose that some boats carry tires as standard equipment to be used as fenders against wharfs or other boats in rafting, but I see no other use for them. Experience has shown that tires tend to bounce and skip along the water unless they are held down with some kind of a weight. Chain tails seem to work well for single or clumped tires.

Among other things, John and Joan Casanova carried two tires aboard their *Tortuga Too* and tried them as drogues several times, but they found the jerky motion of the boat was too uncomfortable. Then they invented the Easter basket tire illustrated in Figure 27. The cutaway tire gave plenty of drag and produced no lift to make it bounce. For obvious reasons avoid steel-belted or radial tires for modification.

The number and size of tires to be towed has never been addressed and I would dismiss the whole idea unless I just happened to have tires aboard for some reason that escapes me at this writing. If the tire drogue works, as some say it does, it has to be a very awkward solution in this day of advanced technology.

Moitessier mentioned towing warps with iron pigs at the free ends. Presumably this was to make an arc in each warp to add drag and also to prevent the warps from being cast forward on a breaking wave. Obviously he wasn't too pleased with his idea for he cut them loose and went surfing instead. But the basic idea has been used by others with only a slight modification. Instead of the iron pigs attached to the warps, ground anchors were used—most likely not lightweight, stock-stabilized, or any other design that tends to kite when towed. It would be hard to predict the performance of such a drag device and it certainly sounds like another makeshift jury rig at best.

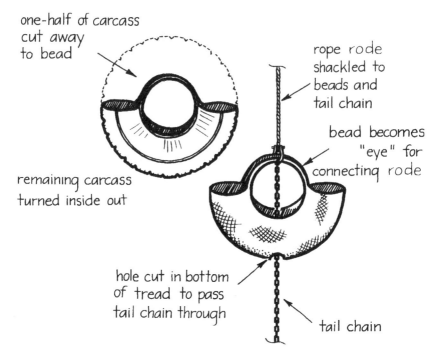

one-half of carcass
cut away
to bead

rope rode
shackled to
beads and
tail chain

bead becomes
"eye" for
connecting rode

remaining carcass
turned inside out

hole cut in bottom
of tread to pass
tail chain through

tail chain

Figure 27. A sophisticated tire drogue.

You have read and heard of successes and failures in the use of jury-rigged drag devices like the foregoing, which may lead you to believe that there is no common thread of application to them. That is not the case. It is clear from the stories that drag devices towed astern when running down large seas are successful *provided that they have enough drag* and that they are attached to the boat in such a manner that *the rudder remains effective.* Unless these criteria are met, it is probably more dangerous to tow the jury-rigged devices than not to have any at all.

RESEARCHED DROGUE DESIGNS

Design criteria for drogues are even less well structured than those for sea anchors. It has been a cut-and-try process on the part of those who wanted the benefits of something called a drogue that they could tow behind the boat when running downwind in heavy seas. Only recently have organized efforts been directed towards quantifying the needs for and the designs of drogues. Drogues can be classified as 'unitary' if they are normally used as a single device on a rode, and 'series' if they consist of a multiplicity of small devices attached to the rode. Among the unitary drogue designs of note which have been well-researched are the Delta, Galerider, Seabrake, Variable Pull, and the SeaClaw drogues. The series drogue is a unique one-design based on the research of Donald Jordan.

JORDAN'S DROGUE RESEARCH

Donald Jordan has done a lot of innovative research on the use of drogues to improve the safety of sailing yachts and life rafts (Jordan 1984, and see *Sail*, June 1986, September 1985, December 1982, and February 1982; and *Multihull*, January/February 1987). His tests were conducted in water tunnels with scale models ballasted to give the proper dynamic characteristics. Breaking waves were simulated with horizontal jets of water, and by the wake of a towed boat. He has identified a number of design and operating considerations pertinent to the use of drogues on boats in survival storms. In summary these are:

- Modern sailing yachts are capable of lying a-hull in large *non-breaking waves* with no significant risk of capsizing.
- A drogue whose diameter is about 10 percent of the boat's length is adequate to hold the stern of a *non-steered boat* into the wind in *non-breaking waves* and will prevent it from surfing down the face of the waves.
- A drogue diameter of more than 10 to 15 percent of the boat's length is required to stabilize it in *breaking waves* when there is no *active steering*.
- If the boat's stern is held *directly into the breaking wave* by *active steering*, a smaller drogue will suffice than if the stern is at a broader angle to the wave. (This is sufficient reason to maintain active steering while running before the seas either with or without a drogue.)
- In a *breaking wave strike*, the drogue must act quickly and powerfully to bring the stern of the boat into the fast moving water of the breaking wave. If the drogue is too small, or the rode is too elastic or has too much slack in it, the boat may broach and capsize.
- Wind does not appear to be a significant factor in the capsizing of a boat. With all sail off, there is little force due to wind pressure, espe-

cially when you consider that the boat is partially shielded from the wind by the wave itself.

This author would caution the reader to be wary of using a high-drag drogue whose diameter is as large as 10 to 15 percent of the boat's length without considerable experimentation in less than gale force winds. Jordan's work assumes non-steered boats at 45° to the breaking waves. It becomes the drogue's job to slue the boat down-wave and hold the stern into the break. This is a very demanding assignment and produces a severe loading on the transom as the wave strikes. Broad, flat transoms (as in an OI-41) are particularly vulnerable. Low, duck-tailed transoms common to modern racing boats (such as the J/41) would be totally inundated, putting crew members who are in the cockpit at extreme risk. (See boat characteristics in Appendix A.)

If the boat can be actively steered downwind and capable helmsmen are available for this, then a drogue under 10 percent LOA would appear to be quite effective.

Estimating drogue size is more nebulous than estimating the size of a sea anchor. With a sea anchor you want to keep the speed low, so having too large a sea anchor is not a problem. But with the drogue, you are seeking a size that will let you sail comfortably downwind and downwave. It will not let you go too fast for your steering ability nor too slow so that overtaking waves pose a threat to your survival. It is obvious that one size of drogue will not be perfect for all combinations of wind speed, boat speed, and sea conditions. But, since it is impractical to carry more than one drogue on a boat, the best "average" size should be selected.

Note in the following descriptions of researched unitary drogues that the drag of the drogue increases significantly as the boat speed increases. At some point the vessel's driving forces (Figure 25) come into equilibrium with the drag forces and the boat speed will be stabilized, however, the variables of the driving forces will never allow it to remain stable for long. Even with a drogue, a good measure of seamanship must be employed because each sea is different and only the crew on board using all of its available resources can successfully bring the boat through stormy seas. You cannot depend solely on mechanical devices to solve all the problems that the ocean can throw at you.

DELTA DROGUE

The Delta drogue is a triangular-shaped device with a small mouth opening and three side vents producing a strong uniform flow at all leading edges. It is inflated by the pressure of the water directed inside through the mouth. The concept was proven by ballute-like drogues used for aerospace recovery systems. The guide surface design insures a strong, uniform airflow separation around the leading edges, similar to that produced by spoilers on race cars. The angled leading edge creates a positive normalizing flow which together with a stable drag force produces a strong stabilizing moment when the drogue is displaced from a zero angle of attack attitude. The small mouth of the drogue makes it highly unlikely that the device will ever get turned "inside out" in tumbling seas.

The Delta drogue is made from heavy (14 oz) vinyl-coated fabric with three bails which are made of heavy nylon webbing and terminate in a single stainless steel swivel. The swivel is provided as a connection to the rode to minimize any possible twisting in the polyester braid rode, a possibly redundant design. The three side vents have a noticeable effect on increasing the drag of the drogue as speed increases. Of all the unitary drogues, the Delta appears to have the highest drag gradient.

The Delta drogue is a three-cornered shape with a central mouth into which water flows to inflate it. At the three corners of the base are radial vents from which the water flows outward. These vents, plus the shaped guide surfaces ahead of them, ensure the drogue's stability under tow. Courtesy Para-Tech Engineering Co.

Deployment of the Delta drogue is made simple through the use of compact stowage bags, one holding the drogue itself and the other holding the rode. These bags are packaged ahead of time (on shore for the first use) and are connected through a short length of exposed rode. During deployment the opening shock is very gradual due to the relatively low speed between deployed drogue and the boat. At full deployment the drag has increased measurably and smoothly to its stabilized drag value.

(a) Delta drogue drag

Drogue size inches		36	48	72	96	114	144
Drag	2 kts	20	54	125	170	200	230
load -	4 kts	70	220	400	710	780	910
lbs at	6 kts	150	500	750	1600	1800	2100
speeds	8 kts	270	N/A	1300	N/A	3200	3700

(b) Delta size selection

Boat size LOA - feet	to 25	to 35	to 45	to 55	to 65	to 80
Drogue size inches	36	48	72	96	114	144
Rode material	Polyester braid					
Rode diameter	1/2 inch			5/8 inch		

Table 5. Delta drogue characteristics. Courtesy of Para-Tech Engineering.

GALERIDER

A unique design approach to a drogue is the Galerider, designed and built by Hathaway, Reiser & Raymond of Stamford, Connecticut. This drogue is, essentially, a paraboloid of 2-inch nylon webbing sewn together on 6-inch centers much like an airplane cargo net. The open nature of the design allowing easy flow-through of the water gives it an inherent stability and it does not oscillate nor yaw in use. The mouth is held open by a circle of 3/8-inch 1 x 19 stainless steel wire in a toroidal spring shape.

Left. The parabolic shape and web construction of the Galerider are clearly shown here. *Right.* The Galerider drogue packs into a neat 2' x 1'6" bag with attaching swivel at the ready. Courtesy Hathaway, Reiser & Raymond.

The Galerider got its initial testing by the 20-ton yacht *Southerly* in a passage from New York to Antigua (*Sailor*, December 3, 1985). Winds reached Force 10 as the yacht sailed into the Gulf Stream and seas became confused. First *Southerly* was reefed, then the jib was removed, and later a trysail was set. As things got worse, the trysail was doused and the boat was allowed to run under bare poles. Speeds ranged from 3 knots on the backside of waves to more that 12 knots on the face, and broaching became a possibility in spite of the helmsman's best efforts.

A 4-foot diameter prototype Galerider was deployed on a 1 1/4-inch nylon anchor rode 200 feet long and belayed to a coffee grinder winch on the afterdeck. (*Southerly* is a center cockpit boat.) The rode was paid out to its full length with no opening shock and the boat soon slowed to a steady 3 knots. As the skipper said, "It went from a charging bull to a docile crea-

(a) Galerider drogue characteristics

Size - diameter x length - inches		30 x 36	36 x 42	42 x 48	48 x 56
Drag	2 kts	17	25	38	54
load -	4 kts	70	100	150	220
lbs at	6 kts	160	230	350	500
speeds	8 kts	280	410	620	900

(b) Galerider size selection

Displacement lbs	to 10,000	10 - 30,000	30 - 50,000	55 - 90,000
Size - diameter x length - inches	30 x 36	36 x 42	42 x 48	48 x 56
Rode material	Double braid nylon rope			
Rode diameter	5/8 inches		3/4 inches	

- Displacements are soft limits. Use the next smaller size drogue if you want the boat to move faster with drogue deployed. Use the next larger size drogue if you want the boat to move slower with the drogue deployed.

- Recommended that powerboats should use one size smaller drogue

- Rode lengths will be discussed in Chapter 7

Table 6. Galerider drogue characteristics. Courtesy of Hathaway, Reiser & Raymond

ture under full control." The helmsman could steer through about 90° and the boat's rolling decreased from full gunnel down on each side to about ±20 degrees. Although several seas boarded the stern, no green water reached the cockpit to threaten the crew. It was estimated that the drogue rode about 30 feet beneath the surface of the water without additional ballast. Finally, it was pointed out that the Galerider drogue was easily winched in with the coffee grinder and lifted aboard by one man.

It is also reasonable to consider rigging these drogues in tandem for boats of even greater displacement. In that case, it is recommended that the short rode for the second Galerider be threaded through the centerline vent hole of the first and attached directly to the shackle holding the first Galerider to the primary rode. The manufacturer recommends that the Galerider should be at least a full sea (wave length) behind the boat to insure that a rogue wave or crest cannot lift both the boat and the Galerider in the same motion.

SEABRAKE

The Australian-developed fabric Seabrake GP, now marketed in the United States, is a variation of the hard-molded plastic cone-shaped Mk 2 which, although quite successful in its own right, suffers from a major stowage problem aboard small vessels. The Mk 2 does have the advantage of being suitable for high speed planing boats. Both versions carry the same name, Seabrake, so identification must be made as GP (soft version) or Mk 2 (hard version).

The GP drogue is made of a synthetic canvas with stainless steel rings sewn inside the leading edges of both cones to provide rigid inlet shapes. Nylon and polyester webbing reinforce the cones and serve as shroud lines to a stainless steel D-ring. The hydrodynamic shape consists of the all-important guide surface in the shape of a truncated cone ahead of a drag-producing cone. The angled guide surface creates normalizing forces which help eliminate the age-old problem of simple conical drogues, namely erratic tracking. When the drogue departs from a zero angle of attack (in any direction), the normalizing force of the guide surface restores its position preventing zigzagging, kiting or fluttering.

At low speeds, water enters the mouth of the truncated cone and exits through the gap between cones and through the apex of the drag cone. At higher speeds, the drag cone apex tends to choke and most of the flow exits

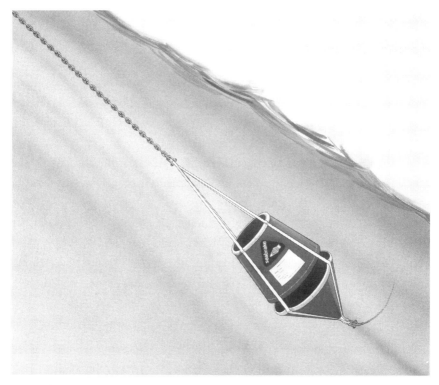

The Seabrake GP collapsible drogue. The GP 24 model folds into a thin pancake-shaped package of approximately 24 inches in diameter and four inches thick. Courtesy Creative Marine Products.

through the gap between cones. Towing tests showed the need for a small weight at the mouth to prevent porpoising (shallow running) and that has been made part of the production design. The drogue has been tested at speeds up to 14 knots although 11 knots is considered the maximum application speed. The Seabrake GP collapsible drogues are designed for displacement, semi-displacement and sailing vessels with hull speeds under 11 knots.

The GP series drogue is provided with a tripline which can be tripped by one person in less than one minute while under tow at one knot. A special model, the GP 24S, is approved by the Australian Maritime Authority for use with lifeboats and the whole GP series is approved by the Australian Yachting Federation as an emergency steering device for boats sailing under its aegis.

(a) Seabrake drogue drag

Model number	GP-24			
Speed - kts	2	4	6	8
Drag - lbs	80	260	570	980

(b) Seabrake size selection

Boat length - feet	to 25	26 - 46	47 - 66	67 - 90
Model number	GP-18	GP-24	GP-30	GP-36
Diameter - inches	18	24	30	36
Rode material	Braided polyester rope			
Rode diameter inches	1/2	9/16	5/8	3/4
Chain size - inches	5/16	5/16	3/8	1/2
Chain length - feet	5	6	8	12
Tripline material	Polypropylene rope			
Trip line diameter - inches	1/4	5/16	3/8	1/2

- Use Proof Coil chain for the lead
- Rode length will be discussed in Chapter 7

Table 7. Seabrake drogue characteristics. Courtesy Creative Marine Products

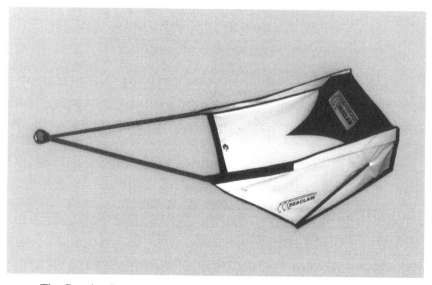

The Coppins Seaclaw is a 'diving' drogue that seeks a depth of 1/6th of its rode length putting it below surface turbulence when in use. It floats to the surface after use. Courtesy W.A. Coppins.

SEACLAW

The SeaClaw is a most unusual drogue being of rectangular shape. It is further a drogue which 'dives' when it is towed taking it to a depth below most of the turbulence of the waves. The depth at which it operates is nominally 1/6th of the length of the deployed rode. Boat speed will be held between three and four knots with a compatibly-sized model. By itself the SeaClaw has no tendency to rotate, however when towed with twisted construction rope, the rope under tension may want to rotate, hence it is equipped with a swivel to prevent twisting together of the two shrouds.

The body of the SeaClaw is made from heavy ripstop PVC, reinforced with webbing. The mouth is kept open by two stainless steel rods top and bottom. Water pressure holds the rectangular bag open. The SeaClaw can be folded up into a compact package after use.

To deploy the SeaClaw, belay the bitter end of the rode to a substantial fitting near the transom with the rode led outside of all stanchions, stays or other gear. Shackle the rode to the swivel making sure the pin is tight and safety-wired. Lay out the rode on deck so that it can deploy freely overboard without getting tangled in any gear. Make sure that all human

Seaclaw size selection

Boat LOA meters	to 10	to 15	to 20	to 25	to 30
Model No.	SC-1	SC-2	SC-3	SC-4	SC-5
Mouth width mm	450	600	700	800	900
Rode material	3-strand or braided nylon (no chain is required to sink the drogue)				
Rode diameter mm	8	10	10	12	14

- Rode length is between 60 and 100 meters

Table 8. SeaClaw drogue size selection. Courtesy W.A. Coppins.

legs are out of the way. Place the SeaClaw in the water with the float up and pay out five to ten meters of the rode snubbing up carefully. Check that the device is diving, then release the remaining rode. When tension comes on the rode the device will dive to its working depth well below surface turbulence.

The SeaClaw does not need a tripline for recovery. Simply remove the tension from the rode and the float will bring it to the surface. Motor up to it and lift it out of the water with a boat hook.

SHEWMON TRUNCATED-CONE DROGUES

The truncated-cone drogue like the Shewmon sea anchor has been extensively developed over recent years and given severe tests to determine its drag performance, strength, and yaw characteristics (Daniel Shewmon, "Drogues, Tires and Warps," *Cruising World*, April 1984). The measured drag performances are shown in Figure 28 for a range of truncated-cone drogue sizes from 2 to 4 feet in diameter. These full-scale drag tests were accomplished by a powerful harbor tug with a pull of 10,000 pounds.

There appeared to be little tendency for the truncated cone drogues to yaw, which is attributed to the through-flow feature of the design, i.e., a vented cone. This appears to be an essential characteristic of any drogue. Venting is a technique used in many aero- and hydrodynamic designs to

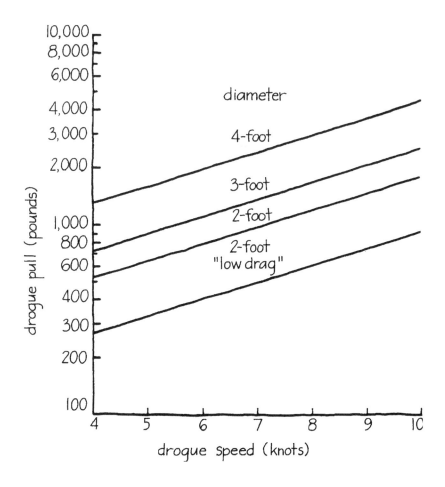

Figure 28. Drag performance of Shewmon truncated-cone drogues. By permission of Shewmon, Inc., ©1986.

stabilize the flow behind an object that is creating oscillatory detached flow. Rotation of the drogue is limited by the use of 3-pound weight sewed along the hem of the canopy opening.

Following are recommendations of Shewmon truncated-cone drogue sizes for different size boats:

Boat LOA (feet)	Drogue diameter (feet)
30	2
40	3
60	4

A 3-foot-diameter Shewmon truncated-cone drogue showing the character-istic large tail opening (vent) of a drogue. In tests this drogue developed over 3,000 pounds of drag at a 7 1/2-knot towing speed. Courtesy Shewmon, Inc.

Using this table for two example boats—the OI-41 and J/41 (see Appendix A), you must do some rationalization in making your selection since both would appear to use the same size drogues based only on boat LOA. The recommended 3-foot drogue would probably be suitable for the OI-41 with its moderate displacement, full keel, and cruising crew. The same size drogue would, however, seem too large for the J/41 with its light displacement, fin keel, and racing crew. For the J/41 a 2-foot-diameter drogue would appear more appropriate. In both instances, if the drag is too great and the boats are moving too slowly for good rudder control, then a small (storm) jib should be raised.

SHEWMON VARIABLE-PULL DROGUES

In 1987 Shewmon came out with a new drogue concept in which the drag can be varied. The drogue body is flat cloth (therefore the name 'seamless'), cut in the shape of a square, hexagon, or decagon depending on its

The 54-inch Shewmon variable-pull drogue is made in the shape of a hexagon with six shrouds connecting it to the tether. Note the trip line at the center. The manufacturer believes this concept will replace the truncated-cone drogue because of its greater efficiency, variable drag feature, and cheaper and more durable construction. Courtesy Shewmon, Inc.

The Shewmon variable-pull drogue undergoing a water test. This 54-inch drogue is partially tripped by the trip line to reduce the water drag on it. The float attached to the trip line extension assures refilling after being tripped. Courtesy Shewmon Inc.

(a) Shewmon Seamless drogue drag (fully opened)

Drogue size inches		27	54	70	106
Drag	2 kts	40	170	530	700
load	4 kts	170	700	2200	3000
lbs at	6 kts	360	1500	4500	6000
speeds	8 kts	700	2800	- -	- -

(b) Shewmon Seamless size selection

Boat size LOA - feet	to 25	25 - 40	40 - 60	60 and up
Drogue size inches	27	54	70	106
Rode material	Nylon double braid			
Rode diameter inches	3/8	5/8	3/4	1
Trip line	5/16 inch nylon double braid			

- Beacause of the drag adjustment possible with the Shewmon variable-pull drogue, one size can handle a span of boat sizes.

- If the boat can be actively steered downwind and capable helmsmen are available for this, then a drogue under 10 percent LOA would appear to be quite effective.

- Rode length will be discussed in Chapter 7.

Table 9. Shewmon Seamless (variable pull) drogue characteristics.

size. The shrouds are attached to the corners of the polygon canopy in a conventional manner but, in addition, there is a trip line attached to the apex of the crown which parallels the tether and runs back to the boat. This trip line can be pulled to invert the canopy from the center, thereby varying the drag of it. In the extreme, the canopy can be turned inside out for retrieval. If the trip line is relaxed, the canopy will refill automatically due to a drag device positioned downstream of the canopy. These drogues are self-opening, seamless, and relatively cheap.

SERIES DROGUE

As a result of his research, Donald Jordan conceived a prototype drogue design suitable for a 30-foot fin keel sailboat (*Sail*, June 1986). His concept, with approximate dimensions, is illustrated in Figure 29. The whole idea of the "series drogue" is to maintain a more or less constant pull by the drogue (a) to prevent the boat from having time to turn sideways to the waves and (b) to prevent the drogue and tether from possibly being cast forward by a breaking wave and becoming tangled and useless. The drogue is weighted to make it run deep, well below wave action and to maintain a small tension in the rode at all times. (Jordan's *Sail* article indicates the use

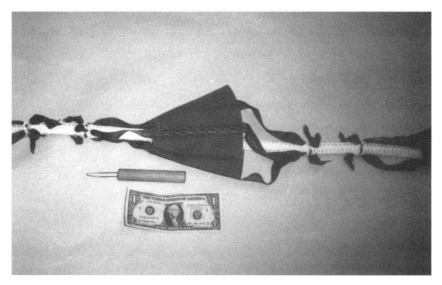

One of the cones which make up a series drogue. The implement for threading the tabs through the braided line is also shown. Courtesy Ace Sailmakers.

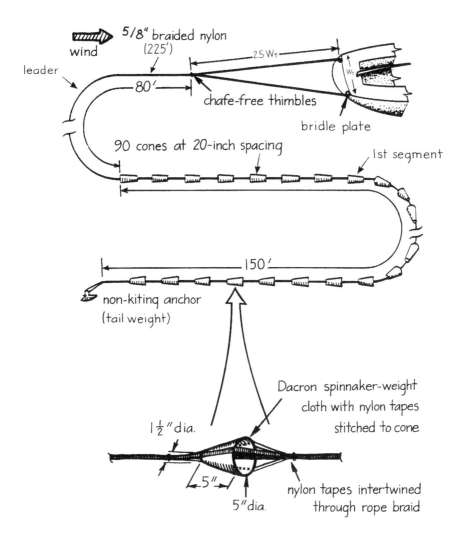

Figure 29. Series drogue by Jordan, sized for a 30-foot LOA fin keel sailboat.

of a stock-stabilized pivoting fluke anchor of 25 pounds or more. This anchor style is known to "kite" when dragged through the water and could induce some unwanted motions at the end of the drogue. I would suggest the use of a non-kiting anchor or a lead weight.)

The series drogue is a fresh approach to attacking the heavy weather survival problem. Consideration must still be given to whether you intend to steer the boat downwind or to let it be completely restrained and con-

(a) For monohulls

Boat displacement - lbs	Number of cones	Rope requirements: diameter (inches) x length (feet) nylon double braid				Tail weight lbs
		leader	1st segment	2nd segment	3rd segment	
10,000	100	5/8 x 75	5/8 x 167	none	none	15
20,000	116	3/4 x 75	3/4 x 97	5/8 x 97	none	15
30,000	132	3/4 x 75	3/4 x 110	3/4 x 110	none	25
40,000	147	7/8 x 75	7/8 x 123	3/4 x 61	5/8 x 61	30
50,000	164	1 x 75	7/8 x 137	3/4 x 68	5/8 x 68	50
60,000	180	1 1/4 x 75	1 1/4 x 187	1 x 94	3/4 x 94	60

(b) For multihulls

Boat displacement - lbs	Number of cones	Rope requirements: diameter (inches) x length (feet) nylon double braid			Tail weight lbs
		leader	1st segment	2nd segment	
6,000	130	5/8 x 75	5/8 x 217	none	15
12,000	140	5/8 x 75	5/8 x 233	none	20
18,000	150	3/4 x 75	3/4 x 125	5/8 x 125	25

- Since series drogues are custom made for each boat, exact details may vary from the numbers given above
- Bridle leg lengths (net) are 2.5 times the width of the transom or distance between outer hulls of a multihull
- Given rope lengths do not include splice requirements

Table 10. Series drogue makeup. Courtesy Ace Sailmakers

trolled by the action of the drogue. If you want to steer the boat when running under a drogue, and are capable of it, then you do not want the series drogue, but a unitary drogue. On the other hand, if you are willing to allow the drogue to take full control of the boat, then the series drogue with a bridle is proper. You had also better be certain that the boat is able to take the full impact of breaking waves on the transom and in the cockpit. Jordan recommends that the crew take refuge below decks, using safety harnesses akin to seat belts to hold crew members safely in their berths.

This is not a scheme to be tried with just any boat since today's boats are structurally unsound for such loadings. Transoms must be heavily reinforced; the cabin structure must be strengthened to resist the tons of water that would descend on it in a breaking wave situation (center cockpit boats would have a great appeal in this situation); the cockpit tub must be made smaller to hold less water and provided with larger drains to assure that the trapped water will quickly run out and not drag the stern down into the next wave; and the bridle attachment plates have to be well backed up with straps to spread the loads through the hull structure much like standing rigging chainplates do.

Jordan in a 1999 advisory to series drogue owners recommended that special bridle plates be installed on the hull sides to carry the ultimate loads as may be imposed on the boat by the bridle when a breaking wave strikes. He offers the following estimated loads for this situation:

Boat displacement	Single bridle load
10,000	5,000 lb.
20,000	10,000 lb.
30,000	14,000 lb.
40,000	17,500 lb.
50,000	21,500 lb.

MAKING YOUR OWN DROGUE

Making your own drogue is certainly within the capability of canvas craftsmen. The techniques are similar to heavy sail making. K. Adlard Coles in *Heavy Weather Sailing* had something to say about the use and construction of drogues. While in a Force 11 gale in the approaches to the English Channel, Coles deployed a "small sea anchor" from his 32-foot sloop *Cohoe*:

> First we experimented with the anchor in the conventional position forward. Here it did no good. The yacht continued to lie broadside to the seas and the anchor laid away on the windward quarter. So we passed the nylon warp aft and made it fast. At the stern it had much

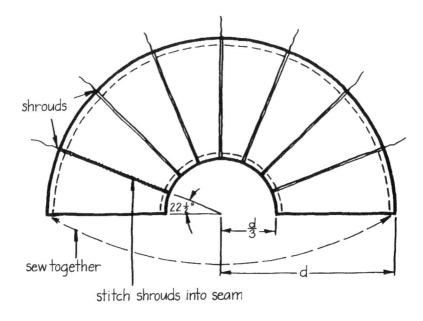

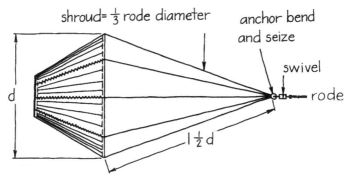

Figure 30. A do-it-yourself drogue design. Reprinted by permission of the publisher, from William G. Van Dorn, *Oceanography and Seamanship*, Dodd, Mead & Company (New York, 1974).

the same result as is achieved by towing warps. It seemed to have a steadying effect, and the yacht lay with the seas on her quarter.

The sea anchor used as a drogue was later lost due to a failure of the ring and Coles adds:

The loss of the sea anchor [sic] confirms the experience of other deep-sea sailing men that tremendous strains are imposed on a sea anchor and its gear, which should be very strong.

Van Dorn in his book *Oceanography and Seamanship* gave the basic design and dimensions for a make-it-yourself drogue. These are reproduced in Figure 30. Particular attention should be paid to strong stitching and quality materials because a drogue takes quite a beating in 24 hours of use, as both Hiscock and Coles noted.

Van Dorn also addressed the size question. He suggested that a truncated conical drogue have a diameter of 1/17th the length of the waterline. For the OI-41 cruising sailboat (34 feet LWL), that would yield a 2-foot-diameter drogue and for the J/41 racing sailboat (36 feet LWL), it would yield a 2.1-foot-diameter drogue. The 2-foot drogue on the OI-41 is, perhaps, small and you might have to lower all sails to keep the boat speed down to a manageable level. On the other hand, the drogue drag may be too great for the J/41. Additional headsail could then be added to keep the boat speed high enough for active steering and to prevent the overtaking waves from having an unnecessarily severe impact on the transom. (See discussion under Shewmon Truncated-Cone Drogues for the same two boats.)

Two other sources of make-it-yourself drogue instructions are contained in *Modern Sailmaking* by Percy Blandford (1978) and *The Finely Fitted Yacht* by Ferenc Mate (1979). In both instances the authors refer to their products as sea anchors when in effect they are too small for sea anchor use, but would make suitable drogues.

CHAPTER SEVEN

Use of Drogues

Running before a sea (sometimes called scudding) is a tactic used by many boats that are structurally sound and fully controllable. It is an exciting and exhilarating ride, but very demanding on the helmsman and the rudder. Running with too much speed can be just as dangerous as running with too little speed. Loads on the rudder (and helm) increase as the square of the boat speed; for example, a speed of 15 knots produces forces 2 1/4 times as great as those at 10 knots. Few boats are built to withstand such forces for long periods of time and few helmsmen can long endure the intense concentration required.

It is the helmsman's job to steer before the waves running off at a slight angle (Moitessier recommended 15°, others suggest as high as 30°) when a breaking crest is about to overtake the boat. Generally you never steer dead down the wave because of the risk of the wave breaking and pitchpoling the boat into the trough. Boats with fine bows, unable to lift, are particularly susceptible to this embarrassing predicament.

Short of pitchpoling, an overtaking breaker may "poop" the boat with sea water by the ton filling the cockpit and finding its way below through loose bin boards, ventilators, broken skylights, etc. The added weight of water and its fluid nature may render the boat marginally controllable and it could quickly take up a position parallel to the waves. There it will be at risk of rolling over if another breaking crest reaches it before the trapped water can be emptied, the boat accelerated, and rudder control reestablished.

Should the helmsman inadvertently steer the boat too broad on the wave, there is the likelihood that a breaking wave will drive the boat into a full broach, dumping tons of sea water onto it while simultaneously rolling it over. Neither the pitchpole nor the broach is an attractive alternative to maintaining full control of the boat running downwind which can be enhanced with the use of a drogue.

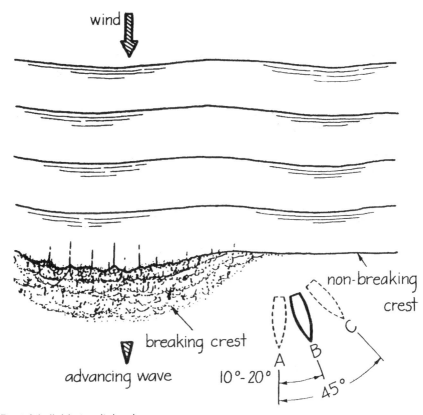

wind

non-breaking
crest

breaking crest

advancing wave   10°-20°

A   B   C

45°

Boat A is liable to pitchpole
Boat C is liable to broach.
Boat B has the best chance at steering survival

Figure 31. Steering angle down a breaking wave.

Speed-limiting drogues are intended to slow the forward speed of a boat and to help keep the stern of the boat directed into the oncoming waves. (The series drogue is a boat-stopping drogue and operates differently from the speed-limiting drogues.) In gales where there is plenty of sea room, it is usually desirable to keep a functioning boat moving and under control, but not to get it in such a position that it will surf down the face of the waves or broach. To avoid broaching, the stern of the boat must be kept 10° to 20° to the waves, for if the boat turns very far off the wave, the crest can slue the stern around, putting the hull broadside to the wave, with the danger of rolling it over. This must be avoided at all costs.

Depending on the wind's speed, you may or may not want to set a headsail—say a Number 4 jib, a storm jib, or a staysail. The idea of a small headsail is to help hold the bow downwind and add some drive for better control. If you have more speed than you can handle just running under bare poles, forget the headsail. But if you do raise one, raise it as high as possible in order that it can see the wind when the boat is in a trough.

The preferred running speed of the boat depends on what the boat and the helmsman can handle. A moderate to heavy displacement cruising boat may ride best at between 5 and 8 knots while a light displacement racing sailboat with a capable helmsman may have a safe, controllable sleigh ride at 10 to 15 knots or even more. If the waves aren't breaking too severely, go for it. If the waves are steep, crisscross, and break frequently, shorten sail, temper your speed to what the helmsman can safely handle, and run before the wind with bare poles and a speed-limiting drogue streamed.

The need for adequate speed when running before the seas was demonstrated by the 42-foot light displacement sailboat *Police Car* in the 1979 Fastnet Race. While running before the gale the crew thought that a speed of 5 or 6 knots was safe until *Police Car* experienced three 120° knockdowns. That was enough to convince them to increase their speed to about 8 knots by changing the trim of their jib. Now the helmsman had enough maneuverability to avoid breaking crests and the boat was no longer victimized by the huge seas (Rousmaniere 1980).

You should note that although a wave may be hundreds of yards or more in width, it will probably be breaking in only one or two places at any one time. Those breaks are what you want to avoid. Take a tip from the board surfer—ride the crest to one side of the break but, unlike the surfer, do not hold your position on the forward face of the wave. Let it pass under you, for if it should break, you will be submerged, just like him, but with poorer chances for recovery.

The idea of the drogue is to slowly pull the boat backwards relative to the wave movement so that it will pass under the boat. Of course, not all boats will react the same to a wave passing under the stern, especially if it is a breaking wave. Broad transoms are most difficult to hold into the wave and long counter sailboats are next in difficulty. Least difficult are double-ended boats, with canoe sterns being the best of all. But good, better, or best, the problem is really one of being able to steer the boat for long periods of time

A typical wave break also has long stretches of unbroken crest on either side which are the places to seek in running downwind with or without a drogue. Courtesy *Latitude 38*.

and to stay alert under the continuous onslaught of overtaking graybeards. Capable helmsmen on racing sailboats are good at this until the point is reached where they become tired, then one miscalculation can spell doom.

John Rousmaniere in his morbidly exciting book *Fastnet, Force 10* describes in vivid detail the harrowing adventures of *Windswept*, an Offshore One Design 34 class that was racing in the 1979 Fastnet Race. Under storm jib alone, with 60 knots of wind, *Windswept* sailed fast and in full control until the mast began shaking violently as the boat was battered by high seas. The skipper ordered the storm jib down and decided to let the boat ride a-hull, a sometimes safe and comfortable technique used by many boats for riding out storms. And so it was for *Windswept* until a huge wave rolled her over, from which she fortunately snapped back onto her feet.

Realizing that lying a-hull was not safe in this maelstrom, the crew improvised a sea anchor which was deployed over the bow on a mooring line. The jury-rigged sea anchor had too little drag to hold *Windswept's* bow into the wind steadily. *Windswept* again fell off until she was broadside to the seas, when another large wave assaulted her and smashed her upside down a second time.

With extensive damage to the boat, an injured crewman, a disabled engine, and a useless life raft, but with the sailing rig still intact, the crew moved the inadequate sea anchor to the stern, making it into what proved to be a lifesaving drogue. The improvised drogue immediately took hold, slowing the boat's downwind rush and making it manageable this time while taking away the threat of a pitchpole.

Windswept's crew tried to improve on the drogue. A 6-gallon jerry can of water provided some drag, but loops of line hung over the stern (warps in a bight) did nothing for the boat. When wind and seas later moderated, the crew took in the improvised but effective drogue, set a Number 2 jib and worked their way to safety at the Crosshaven Yacht Harbor, Cork, Ireland.

Many other boats in the race were in the same predicament as *Windswept* though none, as far as is known, attempted to set a drogue of any sort, but simply hove-to or laid a-hull, tactics which did not work out in the severely confused seas of this gale. In the end 5 boats sank and 19 others had to be abandoned for various reasons. Certainly those that had retained their sailing rigs after the initial roll-down would have had a better chance at survival had they used *Windswept's* drogue technique.

There is an interesting postscript to the Fastnet disaster provided years later by Bill Burrows, chief engineer for the Royal Navy Lifeboat Institution. He helped bring in three disabled Fastnet boats in a 21-hour period of rescue. In an interview with Peter Spectre (*The Yacht*, April 1987) Burrows said:

> Look, you get 300 yachts in poor weather, and you're going to have some in trouble, almost certainly. But the majority of the trouble was hysteria created by the situation and by inexperienced crews. And that it was. They were blaming rudders and such, but none of those rudders would have snapped if they had put drogues out, and storm jibs and run before the weather. They were under bare poles, most of them, and they were getting up on the seas and the seas were about 45 feet, not what we around here call big.
>
> They got up on these seas, and they were running. When the boats were starting to broach, what the helmsmen were doing was hauling on the rudders to stop them from broaching. They were putting too

much bloody strain on the rudders, and they had to go.

Yes, I know they were racing sailors, not cruising men, but that's no excuse. We went out that night and we passed a little old hooker sort of thing with a family of kids aboard, and they were going away to Ireland with no trouble at all.

Now we fast-forward to later years by which time sophisticated, well-engineered speed-limiting drogues had become available and we see a more satisfying picture. The occasion was the 1994 Queen's Birthday Storm and the vessel was the 41-foot cutter, *St. Leger*, with a fin keel, an unbalanced rudder and a Sayes Rig wind vane self-steering system.

Michael and Doreen Ferguson of Canada were passaging between New Zealand and Fiji when the infamous Queen's Birthday Storm developed enveloping them in 50-knot winds. They ran under bare poles in seas described as "very steep and short" while the wind increased with higher gusts. By midnight boat speed had reached 12 knots and they decided that was high enough in those precipitous seas, so they deployed a Galerider drogue on 250 feet of 3/4-inch, 3-strand polypropylene line attached to a cleat on the starboard quarter. The boat speed dwindled to a controllable 3 1/2 to 4 knots and the comfort factor increased significantly.

St. Leger's wind vane self-steering continued to steer all the time. Only one problem developed and that occurred in the troughs of the huge seas when the Galerider would try to catch up with the boat posing a possible fouling of it on the Sayes Rig. Their solution was to shorten the rode to 80 or 90 feet which solved the problem. Then for a total of 60 hours in 60-plus knot winds they continued on their course to Fiji with Sayes Rig doing all the steering. On arrival they inspected the drogue and found it none the worse for wear.

THE STEERING PROBLEM WITH DROGUES

If you have ever towed another boat, you quickly became aware that a tow drastically reduces the maneuverability of your own boat. In fact, if you had attached the towline aft of the rudder it felt like the tail was wagging the dog. Towing principles have been amply demonstrated over the years in tugboat operations and their towing bitts are positioned just aft of the longitudinal center of buoyancy in order to preserve maneuverability. The longitudinal center of buoyancy for a conventional tugboat is generally located at a point 54 to 59 percent of the waterline. That is much too far forward for most recreational boats where deckhouses and other structures would get in the way of an attachment. You may have noticed that tugs avoid this problem by keeping a clear deck aft so that the towline can be brought to the center of buoyancy over the gunnels from the sides as well as from the stern.

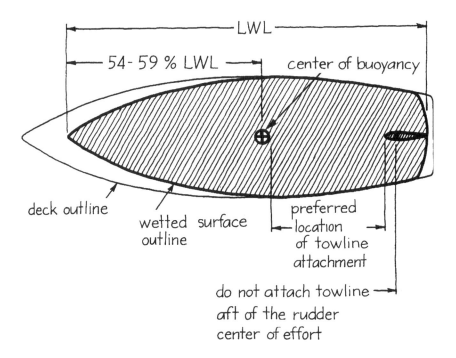

Figure 32. Preferred location for a towing attachment.

One aspect of the *St. Leger* experience is unique and well worth noting. The rode attachment was made at one stern quarter placing it closely abeam of the rudder which was actually doing the steering under control of the Sayes Rig. While the lateral offset location most likely provided some steering torque, it was apparently minimal at the moderate speed the Galerider held the boat to and the rudder was still able to function normally. We do not know the details of their navigation, but it is known that a

Tournament ski boaters have found that placing the towing pylon near the center of the boat greatly enhances maneuverability. If the ski line is attached to an inboard boat as far aft as the transom, it will induce rudder stall. These same arguments say that a drogue should be secured well ahead of the rudder in order for the boat to be able to maneuver when running down-wind and -wave in heavy weather. Photo by the author.

drogue secured to a quarter can provide a modest and useful course trim in one direction or the other.

St. Leger's experience should not be extrapolated freely to other boat designs because we do not know whether their navigation, indeed, favored the added steering torque or not. Furthermore, boats whose quarters are significantly aft of the rudder will experience the tail-wags-the-dog problem and self-steering will be hindered. Admittedly it is difficult to attach the drogue rode ahead of the rudder as in a tugboat and impossible to attach it as far forward as the longitudinal center of buoyancy but all effort must be made to preserve the maneuverability of your boat. When a large graybeard rumbles down on your transom, you will be desperate to square your boat away before it hits, and retaining adequate rudder control is all that will do it. The problem of the drogue fighting the rudder or wind vane steering can be minimized by using a bridle attached to the transom quarters.

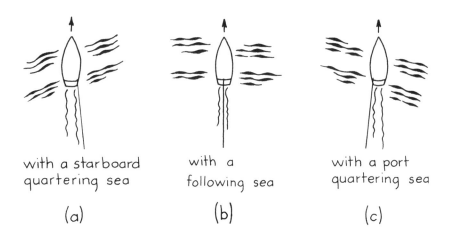

with a starboard quartering sea	with a following sea	with a port quartering sea
(a)	(b)	(c)

• Avoid running with sea directly astern as in (b)

• Whenever possible, steer with a slight quartering as in (a) or (c)

Figure 33. Steering a boat with a unitary drogue attached to a quarter.

STEERING WITH A BRIDLE

One of the features of speed-limiting drogue use which has evolved over the years from practical considerations has been the drogue bridle. If not invented by Donald Jordan in his research (Jordan 1984), it was at least formalized by him in defining the attributes of the series drogue. The concept of the bridle is simple, when the boat veers off its course at an angle to the drogue's pull, one leg of the drogue slackens while the other takes an increased load pulling the boat back on course. A short length bridle makes the more vigorous corrections while a long bridle makes more moderate corrections. The series drogue depends 100-percent on this steering capability, but unitary drogues can use it to supplement their own rudder steering.

Unlike the easy rigging of a sea anchor rode to existing foredeck ground anchor gear, there usually is no substantial ground tackle handling gear at the stern of a boat. The drogue attachment has to make do with what is there. A bridle can take advantage of quarter cleats and headsail winches which usually are positioned symmetrically along the side decks of the

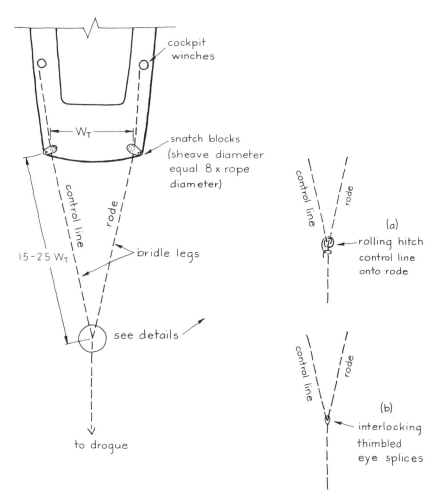

Figure 34. Alternative bridle schemes for a unitary drogue rode.

cockpit. A rope bridle large enough to span the transom is then secured to these cleats and winches with due consideration for preventing chafing.

The ropes making up the bridle should each be of the same material and construction and equal in strength to the rode since as the drogue yaws, either through natural forces or steering effort, its full drag can be applied to one or the other bridle lines. Bridle ropes should be quite long (30-40 feet) so that bridle leg lengths can be freely adjusted later.

RODE DESIGN CONSIDERATIONS

There is a proper rode design for the drogue as there is for a sea anchor rode. It must be long enough to span one wave length (crest to crest distance) at a minimum and be strong enough to withstand the drag load of the drogue—including an allowance for surging. Elasticity is not an issue and some drogue manufacturers recommend polyester material while others recommend nylon material.

Double braid rope construction is commonly recommended for the drogue rode for reasons of its strength, chafe resistance and its anti-rotational capability. It provides a modicum of elasticity to reduce the surge loads on the rode and its attachments to the boat. Too much elasticity, as with 3-strand construction, would render the drogue less effective in sluing the stern of the boat quickly into the breaking wave. The line should be fitted with proper thimbled splices at both ends connecting to the drogue at one end and to the bridle at the other. Some drogue manufacturers provide a swivel as the connection between the drogue shrouds and the rode.

The load applied to the drogue rode is the net of all forces acting on the boat while it is deployed. Those forces identified earlier in Figure 25 are not amenable to simple computation and must come from test data. The test data given in Chapter 6 for the different unitary drogue sizes at different speeds shows that drogue loads can be in the thousands of pounds. Additionally, there can be another 50-percent or so load coming from indeterminate and variable surge loads due to the state of the sea surface (most drag tests are conducted in relatively calm water). The breaking strength of the rope selected for the rode should be twice the estimated total load (test drag plus surge). A larger margin should be allowed if the rode is a piece of rope used for other purposes such as an anchor rode or a utility line whose other uses may have weakened it.

Drogue manufacturers usually have their own ideas on the rode size and material such as were presented in the drogue tables of Chapter 6. A dedicated rode and bridle assembly for the drogue will be a good investment for any boat that regularly operates in the open ocean and must often face gales or worse storms.

DEPLOYMENT AND RETRIEVAL ISSUES

Deployment of the drogue takes place over the stern of the boat after the bridle, rode, and drogue are fully connected to each other and to the boat. The assembly should be carefully checked for proper knots and splices, safety-wired shackles, and freedom from entanglement with itself or any part of the boat and crew when deploying. The rode is deployed when the boat is at a minimum speed starting with the end near the bridle. This is let over the stern so that the drag of the water starts to pull it along in a bight. More and more of the rode is eased over the transom until the drogue, itself, is ready to go. It is then stretched out and cast overboard away from the rode so there is no possibility of it getting tangled. Be aware that the drag of the bight in the rode may produce upwards of 100 to 200 pounds loading. While a strong crewman could handle it with gloved hands, it is advisable to snub it up on a winch or cleat for safety.

There will be an almost imperceptible jerk when the drogue has straightened the rode to its full length, the reason being that the snaking line in the water absorbs most of the shock in straightening itself out. This is particularly true of a properly long rode—one wave length. From that point on, the boat's speed will slow down as the drogue takes hold.

One problem with cone or canopy drogues is their tendency to tumble or flip inside out when the pull on the rode is relaxed. This happens because there is significant backwash of water over it when it slows down due to the boat going into a wave trough when the drogue does not. When the rode again becomes taut, the drogue is snapped back into its streaming position. This continuous snapping of the drogue can place severe strain on the fabric, its stitching, and the rode attachments, leading to early failures unless it was durably built. Drogues such as the Delta and Galerider do not react in this manner.

A more constant load can be obtained if the drogue is made to ride below the surface at such a depth that it is essentially out of the path of the orbiting water particles that make up the wave. To be on the safe side, it would be wise to weight the drogue (or otherwise control the drogue's depth) to about 30 or 40 feet. A few feet of chain between drogue and rode can cause it to ride at a preferred depth (follow manufacturer's recommendations.) There is no simple way to measure the depth at which a drogue is operating, however, knowing how long the deployed rode is, and looking at the angle at which it enters the water, an estimate can be made of the drogue's operating depth. As with the sea anchor, you have to practice deploying the drogue in moderate weather and adjusting its distance astern and its riding depth to assure yourself of its likely behavior and to develop your own technique for handling it. This is vital to its successful use and your safety when the heavy weather is upon you.

Retrieval of the drogue on a sailboat is simple enough if you can use one of the sheet winches to haul it in. Release the control line and haul in on the rode when the boat is in a trough where its speed is slower and the resultant drag load is less. As soon as the drogue's shrouds are within reach, capture one or more with a boat hook, spill the water out of the canopy (if necessary) and then lift it aboard. Remember all the time that water is heavy and water drag can be high. Act cautiously.

Retrieval on a powerboat without winches is more complicated. If you are in calm waters, you can back the boat down to the drogue, being careful not to get the rode caught in the propeller or rudder. The best way, however, is through the use of a trip line if one has been provided with the drogue. This, of course, has to be rigged before deployment. The retrieval method chosen depends not only on the drogue design but on the boat's equipment and the crew's capability, so a little forethought and practice will simplify the operation after the storm.

The operating instructions with the Galerider include the following sage advice: "The complete sequence of attachment, deployment, retrieval and repacking should be tried in moderate conditions. This is the only way to be sure of what to do under storm conditions."

OTHER DROGUE USES

Another use for a drogue is to steady the boat when you are forced to run a breaking inlet. Voss demonstrated this several times, using what he called his sea anchor as a drogue. The action is the same as running before a gale. The drogue slows the boat, keeping the stern into the waves—with help from the helmsman. Slowing the boat not only reduces rudder forces but gives the helmsman more time to think and react—things just don't happen so fast when you are going slower.

The only danger with using a drogue for running an inlet is that it can

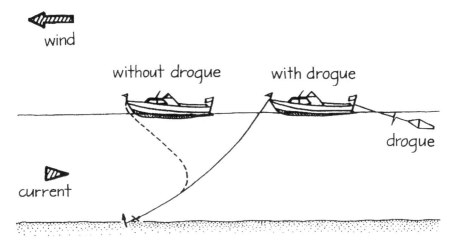

Figure 35. Use of drogue in opposing wind-current situation.

become entangled in rocks, marker buoys, or other hazards surrounding the inlet, especially if the inlet is narrow or has a bend in it. A following breaking sea could also heave the drogue forward threatening to entangle it in rudder or propeller. A sharp serrated-blade knife should be kept handy near the transom to sever the rode should a hang-up occur. By that time, however, the boat may well be far enough inside the inlet that it is no longer menaced by the breakers.

Unlike the sea anchor, which takes full control of the boat when deployed, a drogue takes only partial control. The idea of the speed-limiting drogue is to slow the forward progress of the boat (but not to stop it) and allow the helmsman adequate steering to hold the stern of the boat in a desired position relative to the waves. A series drogue is not recommended for running an inlet.

Captain Richard Friedman of the 60-foot Malahide trawler *Explorer* has other thoughts. In a *Trawler World* web site posting he said:

Do not use a drogue. Most bars are short, have narrow entrances and other traffic. If conditions are such that you are even thinking that a drogue would help, you belong offshore with plenty of sea room.
He added:

Under the right conditions, crossing a bar is no more difficult than entering any harbor. Under the wrong conditions, it can be the most foolish and deadly decision a mariner can make. If you are offshore and conditions have already gone bad, stay at sea and take your lumps.

Should your boat be anchored in a strong current with an opposing wind coming from the stern, it will have a tendency to stand forward on the anchor rode and do more than a little horsing in the stream. One way to eliminate this problem is to deploy a drogue over the stern, getting added drag to hold the boat firmly against the anchor rode as shown in Figure 35.

A boat being towed will often times tend to run up on the stern of the boat doing the towing, due to either following wind and seas or an inadvertent slowdown of the towing boat. To avoid this, the towed boat can trail a drogue, which will add sufficient drag to prevent its momentum from carrying it forward when the towline slackens. If the disabled boat has lost its rudder, the drogue will also stabilize the towed boat directionally, making it easier to be towed. Generally, the towline in a situation like this is quite short. No attempt is made to have one wave length between tower and towee since such tows would be expected to take place in less than breaking seas.

CHAPTER EIGHT

Oil on Troubled Waters

The ability of oil to calm troubled waters is the least studied of all aspects of sea anchoring. Not many people have tried it and there is little unanimity of opinion on how well it works. William Albert Robinson described his experiences (1966) on the 70-foot, 50-ton displacement brigantine *Varua* when she was caught in the "ultimate storm" in the Great Southern Sea of the Pacific Ocean in 1952.

Varua first hove-to under fore staysail and lower main staysail. Fish oil was pumped through the forward toilet and dispersed from bags hanging to windward to form an oil slick, but the boat kept fore-reaching "five or six points" off the wind so the oil disappeared to leeward and was of no help. The sails were subsequently lowered and the wheel fixed amidships, causing *Varua* to lie a-hull with the seas on her quarter. Now the oil became effective because it formed an upwind slick as *Varua* drifted slowly downwind. As the storm further developed, however, things got worse. To quote Robinson:

> The seas were so huge and concave at this point that the whole upper third seemed to collapse and roar vertically down on us. Our oil had little or no effect now, as the surface water was all blown to leeward.

At this point Robinson had to choose another course of action, and this was his thinking:

> It was against prevailing opinion to choose as a last resort to run with the great breaking seas, but I knew instinctively that there would come a point where you could no longer hold her into it, either by drags, sea anchor, riding sails, or any other means. When that point was reached, it would probably be too late to turn and run.

Having tried heaving-to and lying a-hull, Robinson felt that the in-

133

creasing intensity of the storm now demanded that *Varua* run with it. He continues:

> Although under bare poles, *Varua* picked up speed and began running six or seven knots, dangerously, but steering beautifully. We at once put out drags and slowed her down to about three knots, which still left her with good rudder control. It took a seventy-five fathom, two inch diameter manila line which we dragged in a big bight, plus four seventy-five foot mooring lines of the same size, each dragging its big eye splice, plus about a hundred fathoms of associated lines of smaller size. Moving slowly ahead as we now were, we could lay an oil slick right along our path and stern.

The oil slick left behind on the waters with this technique proved quite effective in Robinson's mind.

The quantity of oil dispersed from *Varua* during this storm was quite large and only a vessel the size of *Varua* would have the capacity to carry the required amount. Whereas a small boat may be able to carry sufficient oil for a storm of short duration, it is unlikely that it could carry enough to last several days, which was the case with *Varua*. There is no evidence that a small boat would require any less oil than a large vessel.

The venturesome Capt. Voss used oil when caught in the outskirts of a typhoon in his small boat *Sea Queen* (19 feet LWL). He reported that the oil bags did quite a lot of good in preventing the tops of the seas from breaking off, but as the storm developed further, the oil ceased to help, apparently being blown away or dispersed so much by the turbulent sea that he could see no trace of it on the water.

Another old hand with experience using storm oil was Warwick Tompkins, who brought his schooner *Wanderbird* around the Horn from Gloucester to San Francisco in the early 1930s. Ross Norgrove had met Tompkins and described Tompkin's procedures as follows (Norgrove 1980):

> His method of using oil was simple. He had several dozen bottles, each holding a "fifth" of fish oil, stowed in a locker below decks along with some canvas oil bags. These bags each had a handful of oakum inside (cotton waste will do the same job), and each was capable of holding a bottle of oil. A light line was stitched across the bottom of the bag and up each side, forming a loop at the top; a draw-

string closed the mouth.

To use oil in a gale, all he needed to do was open a bottle, push its neck into the mouth of a bag, and let it glug itself empty; no muss, no skidding around in a pool of oil. Then he pulled the drawstring tight, bent a line onto the loop and, with the *Wanderbird* lying a-hull, pricked the bag with a small spike or ice pick and put it over the windward side on 15 or 20 fathoms of the line. For her 80-foot length, this big, engine-less schooner used two oil bags (one forward one aft), and Tompkins stated that they lasted about 17 hours each. He also told me that lying a-hull with only these two bags out, he seldom even got his decks wet.

Others have carried storm oil aboard their vessels but never used it. Chichester, Smeeton, and Coles are among those sailors. The logistics of carrying storm oil and having it ready for convenient use are a deterrent to having it on board at all.

Whaling by ship has been conducted for centuries and may have originated the idea of using oil to calm waters. The whales were brought alongside the ship where they were 'flensed,' that is, peeled of their blubber. These blubber strips were then hoisted on deck, cut into smaller pieces and 'tried,' that is, boiled to release the oil. During the flensing process, some natural oil dripped from the carcass into the surrounding waters and it was observed to have a calming effect on choppy waters. Spray was reduced making work easier on the flensing stages hanging over the sides near the water. This led to dumping low grade whale oil alongside the mother vessel when launching and retrieving the whaleboats to make transfers less hazardous. In much later years this technique was extended to battleships and cruisers to ease the problems of retrieving seaplanes in the open sea, but by this time less efficient bunker fuel was being used. (*Naval History*, December 1999)

The objective of using oil is to increase the surface tension of the sea, thereby reducing the ability of the wind to ruffle the surface. The effect of oil is greatest on waves in deep water where there is little exchange of water molecules from the surface on down. In shallow waters there is a distinct mixing of surface and subsurface waters, which breaks up the oil film and mixes it with the water.

If waves are not of the mixing variety, only a thin film of oil is required to smooth the surface. In practice, though, there are always some breaking crests that will disperse the oil, requiring that it be replaced in considerable quantity to remain effective. Sea temperature will also have an effect on the oil dispersal since cold waters will tend to thicken the oil, preventing it from spreading into a film over a large area. Fish and vegetable oils will be affected the most and petroleum oils the least.

The best oil for soothing troubled waters, nevertheless, is fish oil, with heavy vegetable oils (raw linseed oil is very good) and other animal oils next on the list. Heavy petroleum oils such as bunker oil and lubricating oil are of average value. Diesel fuel, kerosene, and gasoline are of no value because they spread too thinly, as can be seen in the harbors of the world.

This need for a special oil to be carried in quantities of tens of gallons makes it unattractive to keep in a small boat's inventory of supplies. In dire circumstances a boat could consider using its spare engine lubricating oils but even these are normally not carried in large enough quantities.

The means for dispersing storm oil is another detractor from the use of oil to calm storm-wracked seas. Voss and others have described the traditional storm oil bag which can be kept empty until ready for use. The bag has a capacity of 3 or 4 pints and can be made of No. 2 canvas or 3-ounce Dacron with securely stitched seams. When it is to be used, the bag is stuffed loosely with oakum (what boat carries oakum on board nowadays?), cotton, kapok, or cotton waste and then filled with the available oil. A number of holes should be punched in the bag with a coarse sail needle or marlinspike to assure adequate seepage but not a heavy flow. The bag can be triced over the windward rail or attached to the sea anchor if one is being deployed.

The dispersal technique used by *Varua* (and a much more practical one) is to pump small quantities of storm oil through a water closet. The rate of flow will have to be arrived at by trial and error and one source recommends a tablespoon every few minutes. Not everyone, though, is going to appreciate the smell of oil below decks when the hatches are closed in a storm situation.

If you have lubricating oil in cans on board, you can punch a couple of small holes in them and hang them one at a time in a mesh bag over the side so each can drip its water-calming contents into the slick created by the hull, but don't expect too much from this oil.

A Coast Guard design for a sea anchor with a built-in dispersal can is shown in Figure 36. The diameter at the mouth is 36 inches and it is approximately 54 inches long with a 1-gallon storm oil container. This would be a very awkward item to stow on board, to say nothing about storing additional storm oil. Incidentally, to replenish the storm oil container would require tripping the sea anchor and bringing it back aboard the vessel for refilling and then deploying it once again. Under storm conditions this would seem to be an impractical matter.

Voss noted in his book that there can be other problems with the use of storm oil. Fish oil has a repulsive odor and, if the oil is blown back on the deck or into the cockpit, it can get things dangerously slippery. One should also note that there may be a mess to clean up after the blow; but if you are able to concern yourself with the mess, then you have survived and all is well.

The basic objective in dispersing storm oil is to get it to windward of the struggling vessel and then keep the vessel in the oil slick as much as

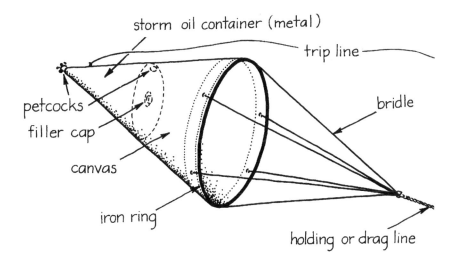

Figure 36. A commercial ship's lifeboat sea anchor. From U.S. Coast Guard *Manual for Lifeboatmen, Able Seamen, and Qualified Members of the Engine Department.*

possible. A rescue vessel to windward of a stricken vessel could dispense oil downwind, hopefully easing the impact of the waves on the stricken vessel, as well as making rescue efforts easier. Onshore waves with an offshore wind could defeat the use of oil in a stranding rescue even though the waves are not breaking heavily. Storm oil dispersal techniques must, obviously, be tailored to the situation and no hard and fast rules can be made.

Finally, one should remember that the discharge of oil at sea from a vessel is in violation of U.S. Coast Guard regulations. However, in an emergency with life and property at risk, it is doubtful whether you should let this technicality stand in your way. The loss of the vessel would free all of the oil in the vessel, causing a somewhat greater ecological and financial calamity.

Afterword

It is interesting to compare the experiences of two single-handed sailors, each in his own bid to circumnavigate the earth with a personal record in mind. Raphael Dinelli at age 28 was participating in the 1996-97 Globe Vendee single-handed race around the world in his state-of-the-art 60-foot LOA *Algimouss*. His troubles started in the Great Southern Ocean between the Cape of Good Hope and Australia, a region known as the Roaring Forties which has been the downfall of many a boat. Huge following seas had been pummeling *Algimouss* as it proceeded towards Australia but then a rogue wave of unusual proportions caught up with her just before Christmas. It grasped *Algimouss* on its breaking face and sped it forward in a manner only a surfer could love. Dinelli knew he was going too fast, but he had no way of slowing down, he did not have a braking device aboard. The ultimate result was a pitchpole, the bow of the boat driving ahead into the next trough. The mast broke and became a battering ram which shattered the hull and shortened the boat's life. The story ends with *Algimouss* sinking and Dinelli being rescued by a fellow race entrant, all for want of a drogue.

The other single-handed sailor had set out in 1995 in quest of the record for the youngest person to circumnavigate the world alone. He was 20-year old "BJ" Caldwell. His record would depend on him completing the course while still under age 21. BJ wisely carried both a sea anchor and drogue for help aboard his 20-year old 26 foot cutter *Mai Miti Vavau*. While Caldwell did not sail in the "Roaring Forties," he found it to his advantage to use his drogue for about 10,000 of the 27,000 sea miles sailed. He found that it restrained his boat speed as following seas attempted to boost him along at uncontrollable surfing speeds. The drogue also served to dampen yawing and prevent broaching such that his stern was always aligned with the oncoming seas to the extent he could even make coffee in comfort when running with the seas. And all the while his alter ego helmsman, a self-steering vane, was able to handle *Mai Miti Vavau*'s steering needs 24 hours a day in large following seas. He did set his record and returned to port with his boat whole.

Although these experiences of two intrepid sailors are distances apart in time, geography, and boat technology, one has to wonder whether Dinelli might have survived that wild, uncontrollable ride down the face of a breaker had he been using a modern drogue at the time. Throughout Victor Shane's *Drag Device Data Base* (1999) one finds a surfeit of examples of boats using drogues to moderate running speeds in heavy weather suggesting that the Dinelli question should be answered in the affirmative. In terms of dollars, space, and weight, a drag device is like a stash of gold—small and valuable.

Of course racing boat skippers don't like to slow their boats down for anything, but in order for them to win the great race, they must also finish which means having a big bag of survival tricks aboard. Racing is not such a blood thirsty affair that boats and crews should be forced beyond the margin of safety. Following the ill-fated Sydney-Hobart race the Cruising Yacht Club of Australia's Review Committee (CYCA 1999) had this to say: "The Committee's investigation into drogues, sea anchors and parachute anchors or a makeshift alternative, shows their use would have been a sound option in the conditions of the 1998 race."

By and large cruisers have learned to give with the weather and not to imperil boat and crew for the sake of a challenge. To them safety of crew and boat in unknown seas and weather is paramount to completing the cruise of a lifetime. They view a temporary sacrifice in speed as an insignificant factor in completing a passage. On the other hand, we still have some macho cruisers, many of whom have learned their sailing skills in earlier racing competition, that still believe anything short of fast compromises safety. They may be right in their own views as most involve larger, custom-built boats and significant investments. Their cases are weakened, however, by the losses previously cited where many race-trained sailors in custom boats suffered tragedy because the weather still climbed one notch higher than they could handle. Having the option to use a drag device makes itself well-known to all at that point.

You should not think of the sea anchor or drogue as an "either/or" device. Even in moderate weather the skipper may simply want to park his boat and rest for awhile, make repairs, or go fishing. Taking way off the boat renders it uncontrollable and the boat, regardless of kind, will seek a position parallel to the waves, creating a very uncomfortable ride. A sea anchor will tend to pull the bow of the boat into the wind and make life aboard more pleasant while parked. Occasionally a boat may encounter a small gale (far from being a survival condition) and, rather than fight it for hours or days on end, the skipper can ride to a sea anchor in relative comfort.

Drogues, however, are rarely used until the storm reaches a near-survival intensity. Then, if the boat remains controllable and the crew capable, it can continue to sail downwind with a drogue moderating its surfing tendency on the face of a wave which could threaten a pitchpole often fatal to the boat and sometimes to the crew. In the ultimate storm you may even elect to turn full control of the boat over to the powerful series drogue for survival. The options available to the skipper are many depending on how well he has equipped his boat.

The large variety of drag devices on today's market, when used with proper seamanship, could give your boat the edge in a survival storm and their prices are modest by any measure. Consider the hull insurance on a $150,000 boat, the approximate cost of an average cruising boat. Insurance premiums would be roughly $4,500 per year. For one-third of the first year's premium you could add either a drogue or sea anchor system that will give your boat a gale (or stronger) survival capability. Which would you rather have when you are 1,000 nautical miles to sea and the weather starts to overcome you—an insurance policy to make your heirs comfortable or a proven drag device for your own survival? You want to be able to successfully meet the challenge of the storm, so give the drag device a chance to show its capabilities. You have lost nothing and in all probability you have saved the day.

To sum it all up—preparation, practice and patience are required to enjoy the benefits of a drag device, but first you have to have one onboard. Forward planning is essential.

Estimating Sea Anchor Size

An analytical approach to sizing a sea anchor matches the wind drag of the boat to the water drag of the sea anchor. Since the sea anchor requires a little drift to develop holding power, it will slowly move to leeward, but at such a small relative rate as not to affect the wind drag above the waterline.

At the present there is no closed analytical solution to determining sea anchor size, but there are several estimating techniques which can suffice until more knowledge is obtained. These sizing techniques are referred to here as the *"wind loads method," "equal areas method," "average draft method,"* and *"Van Dorn's method."* All of them are approximations at best, but in the absence of more rigorous methods, they will have to do.

WIND LOADS METHOD

One can design a sea anchor using the wind loads estimating technique developed in my book on ground anchoring (Hinz 1999). At sea anchor, a boat will experience leeward drift since the sea anchor does not have a positive grip on the water such as the ground anchor has on terra firma. This leeward drift is predominately due to the more or less steady pressure exerted by the wind on the hull, superstructure, and rigging. Non-breaking waves tend to produce a fore and aft oscillatory movement of the boat with little net change in position. The impact of the waves is absorbed by the elastic nature of the rode which, when it recovers with the boat on the backside of the wave, actually brings the boat near to its previous location.

If there is no leeward drift of the boat at sea anchor, then the sea anchor will simply float suspended in the water like a huge jellyfish. It has to have motion to develop a drag force and for design purposes you can safely assume 1 knot of leeward drift (V_d) in using Shewmon's data of Figure 10 (Chapter 3).

The aerodynamicist has given us various tools to estimate the wind loads on a boat at sea anchor. One method is to measure them in a wind tunnel, which few of us can afford to do. Another way is to estimate wind loads mathematically based on test data for other boats, for other vehicles such as automobiles and airplanes, and on a whole variety of components which make up a vehicle. The latter method will be described here as it can be done for most boat shapes using a simple hand calculator and the drawings of the boat. (A more complete discussion of determining the wind loads on an anchored boat is given in my book, *The Complete Book of Anchoring and Mooring* [Hinz 1999], from which this section is excerpted.)

The equation for the aerodynamic drag of an object in a wind stream is:

$$D_w = q \cdot C_d A \qquad\qquad [\textit{Equation A-1}]$$

where D_w = drag force (pounds)
q = dynamic pressure (pounds per square foot)
C_d = drag coefficient (dimensionless)
A = characteristic area (square feet)

Values of dynamic pressure q for a range of wind speeds at sea level are:

V(knots)	Beaufort Number	q (pounds per square foot)
10	3	0.33
20	5	1.3
30	7	3
40	8	5
50	10	8
60	11	12
70	12	16
80	13	21
90	15	27
100	16	33

The drag coefficient C_d comes from wind tunnel test data (Table A-1) and is applicable to similar body shapes at different wind speeds as long as the flow is incompressible, which is the case for wind speeds of interest here. These drag coefficients are for 0° angle of attack and 0° angle of yaw. The drag coefficients for boats include a nominal allowance for rigging, lifelines, and antennas.

Vehicle	C_d with wind ahead
Angular tramp steamer	1.2
Cabin cruiser	1.0
Long-liner	0.9
Oil tanker	0.85
Modern ocean liner	0.7
Cruising trimaran	0.6
Cruising catamaran	0.55
Modern automobile (sedan)	0.52
Racing trimaran	0.45
Modern automobile (fastback)	0.34
Ultrastreamlined playboat	0.2
Racing automobile	0.17
Airplane	0.09

Table A-1. **Typical vehicle wind drag coefficients.***

*Source: T. Baumeister, ed. *Mark's Standard Handbook for Mechanical Engineers*, 8th ed. New York: McGraw-Hill Co., 1978; and William F. Durand, ed. *Aerodynamic Theory*, vol. 4. Gloucester, MA: Peter Smith, 1976.

The author calculated a number of additional drag coefficients for monohull sailboats of differing displacement/length ratios:

$$\frac{D}{L} = \frac{\text{displacement (long tons)}}{(.01\ \text{LWL})^3} \qquad [Equation\ A\text{-}2]$$

where LWL = waterline length (feet)

These correlated well with the displacement/length ratios of the hulls (Figure A-1).

The characteristic area A is the area of the body measured perpendicular to the wind. The drag D_w of a body is proportional to the area of the body allowing scaling of drag forces for bodies of different size but same shape. Boats, however, have been observed to veer as much as 30° from side to side when anchored. Therefore, the characteristic area to be used for wind drag load calculations is the yawed area presented to the wind when the angle of yaw reaches 30°. One could also make a correction for the drag coefficient at an angle of attack but this becomes of secondary importance if the characteristic yawed area has been used.

The wind drag load on a boat yawed at 30° to the wind becomes:

$$D_w = q \cdot C_d \cdot A_{30°} \qquad [Equation\ A\text{-}3]$$

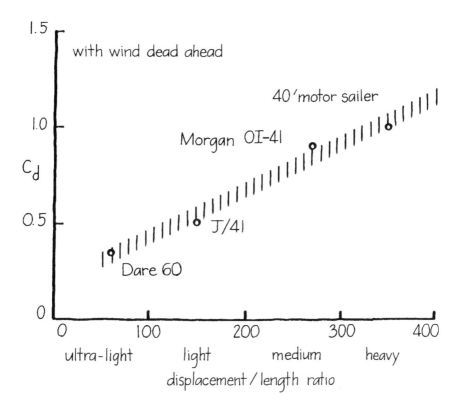

Figure A-1. Monohull sailboat wind drag coefficients.

Having determined the wind drag of the boat at a given wind speed, you then enter the graph of Figure 10 (Chapter 3) and determine the size of sea anchor needed to hold the leeward drift to your chosen value.

    Example: The Uniflite Coastal Cruiser powerboat (Figure A-2) has the following applicable dimensions:

        Drag coefficient (C_d) = 1.0
        Characteristic yawed area ($A_{30°}$) = 226 square feet

The drag force on this boat yawed 30° in 60 knots of wind is determined from Equation A-3 as:

        D_w = 12 x 1.0 x 226 = 2,700 pounds

This is the amount of drag that the sea anchor must counter. For a designed leeward speed of 1 knot, Figure 10 (Chapter 3) shows us that the sea anchor must be 9 1/2 feet in diameter (inflated).

If we designed for only 45 knots of wind, the drag would be 1,500 pounds and the inflated sea anchor diameter would be 7 feet. Thus you can design your own sea anchor to match whatever you consider the highest wind speed that you will encounter. *Remember that a larger sea anchor will work at lower wind speeds but a smaller sea anchor may put your boat in jeopardy at higher wind speeds.*

If you have previously designed a ground anchor rode for your boat according to my anchoring book, then you can assume that the wind load D_w for the foregoing calculation is one-fourth of the breaking strength of the selected ground anchor rode and you do not have to repeat the wind load calculation of Equation A-3. Since the boat is being faced with winds of the same magnitude in both ground and sea anchoring situations, the resulting wind loads are the same. (Note: The leeward speed of a boat at sea anchor should be less than 1 or 2 knots and is insignificant compared to the wind speed.) The factor of four in the strength of anchor rode assures sufficient margin for the rode of the same size to take care of wave impact and other variables. The length of the sea anchor rode, however, will probably differ from that used in your ground anchor tackle. This was covered in Chapter 4.

There is an advantage to calculating your sea anchor loads rather than guessing at them and it is that you also have the basis for determining the

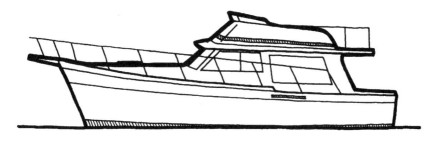

LOA   37 feet, 9 inches
Beam   12 feet, 9 inches
Draft   3 feet, 10 inches

Figure A-2. Uniflite Coastal Cruiser

size of the rode and the associated connecting elements between the sea anchor and boat.

EQUAL AREAS METHOD

We have another hypothesis that says the sea anchor must be large enough to bring the bow of a boat lying broadside to the wind in a trough into the wind. This situation is illustrated in Figure A-3. The turning torque produced by the sea anchor must be greater than the counter torque produced by the wind drag acting forward of the center of lateral resistance. That is:

$$D_{sa} \times \ell_2 > D_w \times \ell_1$$

The greater this differential, the faster the boat will be turned bow-on to the wind and wave. If we assume that the turbulent unit drag of the sea anchor and boat underbody are the same, then we can simply equate the area of the sea anchor to that of the underbody and come up with a first approximation of the required sea anchor size. The differences in lever arm lengths ℓ_1 and ℓ_2 assure that the sea anchor-induced torque will be greater than the wind load torque and that the bow will be pulled into the wind.

Once into the wind, the sea anchor will have more than enough drag to brake the leeward drift to 1 or 2 knots or less.

This equal area sea anchor sizing technique is easy to do, using a copy of the designer's profile view of the boat to determine the underbody silhouette area, and converting that to an equivalent circular area. The circular area of the sea anchor is converted to a diameter by the relation:

$$d_{sa} = \sqrt{4A_u/\pi} \qquad\qquad [\textit{Equation A-4}]$$

where d_{sa} = inflated diameter of the sea anchor (feet)
A_u = measured area of underwater profile of boat (square feet)

Example: The Out Island 41 medium displacement sailboat shown in Figure A-3 has the following applicable dimension:

$$A_u = 103 \text{ square feet}$$

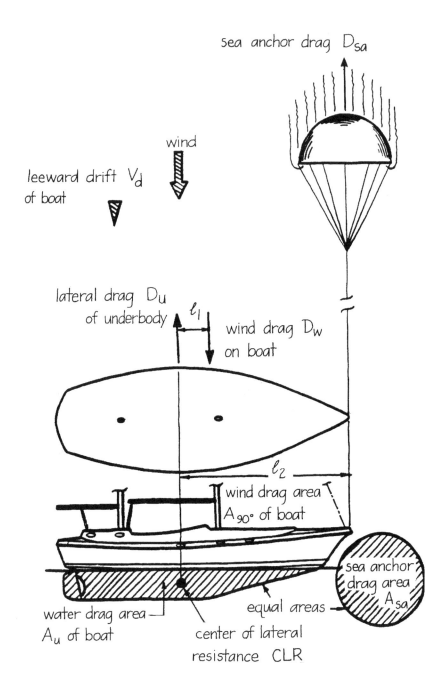

Figure A-3. Equal areas sea anchor sizing method (OI-41).

Therefore:

$$d_{sa} = \sqrt{4 \cdot 103 / \pi} = 11 \text{ feet (inflated diameter)}$$

This is a substantial diameter, necessitated by the long keel which actively tends to resist turning as the sea anchor brings the bow of boat into the wind. Once the bow of the boat is head to wind, a sea anchor diameter of only 9 1/2 feet (based on the wind drag method) would be required to hold it there provided some mizzen sail is set to help weathercock the boat into the wind.

AVERAGE DRAFT METHOD

Shewmon, Inc., recommends a special method for determining the diameter of their sea anchor for use on a modern fin keel sailboat. Since fin keel boats can pivot so easily about their narrow deep keel, the sea anchor needed to turn them into the wind can be smaller than that required for a long keel boat. In equation form the Shewmon recommendation is:

$$d_{sa} = 2 \left[\frac{\Delta A_k}{1/2 \text{ LWL}} + \text{hull draft} \right] \qquad [\textit{Equation A-5}]$$

where d_{sa} = diameter of Shewmon sea anchor (feet)
ΔA_k = broadside area of fin keel (square feet)
LWL = waterline length (feet)

Example: The J/41 light displacement sailboat shown in Figure A-4 has the following applicable dimensions:

$$\Delta A_k = 31 \text{ square feet}$$
$$\text{LWL} = 36 \text{ feet}$$
$$\text{hull draft} = 1.8 \text{ feet}$$

Therefore:

$$d_{sa} = 2 [31 \div 36/2 + 1.8] = 7 \text{ feet (inflated diameter)}$$

If the sea anchor diameter had been determined by the equal areas method, it would have been 10 1/2 feet in diameter—unnecessarily large. If the sea anchor size had been determined by the wind drag method, it would be only 5 feet in diameter because of the streamlined nature of this racing boat.

Shewmon, Inc., in published material dated April 1987, suggests using the following sizes of their sea anchors based on the average draft of

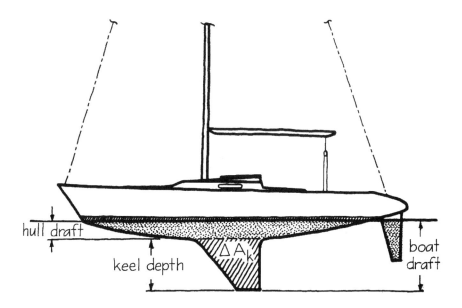

Figure A-4. Profile of a light displacement ocean racing sailboat (J/41).

the fin keel boat as determined by the preceding method:

Boat draft (feet)	*Sea anchor diameter (feet)*	*Rode diameter (inches)*
2	4	9/16
3	6	3/4
4	8	7/8
6	12	1 1/8
7 1/2	15	1 1/4
9	18	1 3/8

The manufacturer should be consulted before ordering any sea anchor, so that he can match a sea anchor size to your specific boat's configuration.

VAN DORN'S METHOD

Another method for estimating sea anchor size was developed by Van Dorn in his book *Oceanography and Seamanship* (1974). He offers an approximate solution to the sizing problem based on the waterline length of the vessel (assumed to be a monohull). His "optimum" sea anchor size is related to the wind speed at which you feel the need to sea anchor. At a wind speed of 30 knots Van Dorn suggests a sea anchor diameter equal to 16 percent of the waterline of the boat. This increases to 25 percent of the waterline for winds of 60 knots. Table A-2 is a numerical representation of his argument for drift speeds of less than 2 knots.

You can make your selection from this table based on the maximum winds that you expect in your area of operations. Obviously, if you design for the lower wind speeds, your sea anchor will be smaller and less expensive but not as good insurance as a larger sea anchor. Your navigator should note that the drift speed V_d is relative to the water, which itself may be moving and must be taken into account in dead reckoning. It is recommended that any boat that operates in blue water have a sea anchor capable of handling 60 knots of wind.

Sea anchor size is determined in the Van Dorn method by the formula:

$$d_{sa} = (f_{LWL})\, LWL \qquad\qquad [Equation\ A\text{-}6]$$

where d_{sa} = uninflated diameter of sea anchor (feet)

f_{LWL} = ratio of sea anchor diameter to waterline length
(Table A-2)

LWL = waterline length (feet)

Example: A sea anchor is desired for the Out Island 41 medium displacement sailboat to handle winds of 60 knots. What should its size be?

LWL = 34 feet   From Table A-2: $f_{LWL} = 0.25$

Therefore:

$d_{sa} = 0.25$ x $34 = 8\ 1/2$ feet uninflated (6 feet inflated)

f_{LWL} (ratio of uninflated sea anchor diameter to waterline length)	Wind speed V_w (knots)		
	30	45	60
0.16	1.3 kts	2.1 kts	2.7 kts
0.21	1.2	1.6	2.2
0.25	0.9	1.3	1.8

Not recommended due to too high a drift speed

Van Dorn's optimum size recommendations

Table A-2. Relative drift speed V_d based on Van Dorn's optimum sea anchor size (exclusive of current).

This is a smaller diameter than either the equal areas method (11 feet) or the wind loads method (9 1/2 feet).

If we look at the J/s41 light displacement sailboat, we see that it has the following applicable dimension:

LWL = 36 feet

Therefore:

d_{sa} = .25 x 36 = 9 feet (uninflated) or 6.3 feet (inflated)

This is in reasonable agreement with the average draft method (7 feet).

After reviewing these several methods of estimating sea anchor size, you are still left with the dilemma of deciding which method will give the best estimate for your boat. There is no single method best suited to all boats, but if you look at your boat's predominant design feature, you can use the method that best takes it into account. For example:

Design feature	*Matching method*
Long-keeled monohull sailboats; displacement and deep-V powerboats	equal areas (conservative) or wind drag
Flat bottom planing powerboats	wind drag
Fin keel sailboats	average draft or Van Dorn's

In making the choice keep in mind that a larger sea anchor assures a more positive grip on the sea, while a smaller sea anchor may let the boat yaw excessively and drift astern too fast for rudder safety.

APPENDIX B

Drag Device Sources

Ace Sailmakers (series drogue–kit or assembled)
  128 Howard Street
  New London, CT 06320
  (860) 443-5556
  www.acesails.com

Cal-June, Inc (trolling & lifeboat sea anchors)
  P.O. Box 9551
  North Hollywood, CA 91609
  (818) 761-3516

W.A. Coppins Ltd. (sea anchors and SeaClaw drogue)
  255 High Street
  Motueka
  New Zealand
  (64-3) 528-7296

Creative Marine Products (Seabrake drogue and Sea Bucket)
  P.O. Box 2120
  Natchez, MS 39121
  (800) 824-0355
  www.creativemarine.com

Fiorentino Para Anchor (sea anchor)
  1048 Irvine Avenue, #489
  Newport Beach, CA 92660
  (800) 777-0732
  www.paraanchor.com

Hathaway, Reiser & Raymond (Galerider drogue)
  184 Selleck Street
  Stamford, CT 06902
  (203) 324-9581
  www.hathaways.com/galerider

R.D. Mengler (sea anchors)
  81 Guthrie Street, Unit 1
  Osborne Park
  Western Australia 6017
  (09) 244-1534

Para-Anchors International (sea anchors, drogues)
  P.O. Box 19
  Summerland, CA 93067
  (805) 966-0782
  www.dddb.com

Para-Tech Engineering Co. (Para-Tech sea anchors, Delta drogue, Boat Brakes)
  2117 Horseshoe Trail
  Silt, CO 81652
  (970) 876-0558
  www.seaanchor.com

Sailrite (series drogue kits)
  305 West Van Buren Street
  Columbia City, IN 46725
  (219) 244-6715
  www.sailrite.com

Shewmon, Inc. (sea anchors, Seamless drogue)
  1000 Harbor Lake Drive
  Safety Harbor, FL 33572
  (813) 447-0091
  shewfla@aol.com

Glossary

Barber haul: A pendant used to haul a line to one side of its normal direction of pull. May or may not be fitted with a pulley block.

Bridle: A rigging of two or more lines attaching a single object to another line; a means of distributing a load by multiple lines.

Broach: To veer or yaw dangerously, especially in a following sea, so as to lie beam-on to the waves.

Canopy: The conical or spherical cloth element of a parachute.

Capsize: To roll more than 90° in the water. Less than 90° is usually referred to as a knockdown.

Chafe: Wear on a line or piece of fabric caused by rubbing contact with another object.

Chafing gear: Any material used to prevent rope or fabric wearing away when in contact with a solid object.

Crown: The apex of a conical or spherical parachute canopy.

Drogue: A drag device attached to the stern of a boat to slow it down.

Gore: A tapered or triangular segment of a rounded surface.

Lie-to: To keep the bow of a boat into the wind with a sea anchor.

Oil bag: A fabric container for carrying and dispersing storm oil during storm conditions.

Para-anchor: A sea anchor made out of, or like, an airman's parachute.

Pendant: A short or moderate length of line connecting an auxiliary object to a primary piece of gear.

Pitchpole: The most disastrous of boat movements—when a boat digs its bow into the water and goes end over end.

Rode: The line connecting a sea anchor or drogue to the vessel.

Sea anchor: A drag device attached to the bow of the boat to essentially "anchor" the boat to the surface of the water with the bow held to windward.

Seaway: The composite shape of the ocean surface caused by a combination of ripples, gravity waves and swells.

Shrouds: The multiplicity of small lines connecting the canopy of a sea anchor or drogue to the rode.

Slick: The smooth water left to windward as a boat moves to leeward.

Spanker: A fore and aft sail set on the sternmost mast of a ketch or yawl (or backstay of a sloop/cutter).

Storm oil: A special oil to increase the surface tension of the water and reduce the ability of the wind to ruffle it.

Tether: The line that connects a specialty sea anchor to the gear it is tending.

Trip line: A smaller line that connects the apex of a sea anchor or drogue to the vessel and is used to "trip" or unload the drag device.

Vent: The opening at the apex of a conical or spherical drag device that permits the escape of water and, thereby, stabilizes the device as it is towed through the water.

Yawing: The angular motion of a boat about its vertical axis. When the boat yaws, its bow and stern swing from side to side. Sometimes called sheering when at anchor.

Bibliography

Bitting, Kenneth R. *The Dynamic Behavior of Nylon and Polyester Line*. Report No. CG-D-39-80. Washington: U.S. Coast Guard, 1980.

Blandford, Percy W. *Modern Sailmaking* (TAB book number 397). Blue Ridge Summit, PA: TAB Books, Inc., 1978.

Bowditch, Nathaniel. *American Practical Navigator*. Pub. No. 9. Washington, DC: Government Printing Office, 1958.

Casanova, John and Joan, et al. *The Parachute Anchoring System and Other Tactics*. Boston, MA: Chiodi Advertising and Publishing Co., 1982.

Claughton, Andrew. *Report on Model Tests to Assess the use of Drogues and Similar Devices to Prevent Yacht Capsize in Breaking Waves*. Ship Science Report No. 35. Southampton, England: University of Southampton. 1988.

Coles, K. Adlard. *Heavy Weather Sailing*. Camden, ME: International Marine Publishing Co., 1991.

Cruising Yacht Club of Australia. *Report of the 1998 Sydney-Hobart Review Committee*. Darling Point, Australia: CYCA, 1999.

Dashew, Steve and Linda. *Surviving the Storm*. Tucson, AZ: Beowulf, Inc. 1999.

Forbes, Sir Hugh, et al. *1979 Fastnet Race Inquiry*. London, England: Royal Ocean Racing Club. 1979.

Gershon, Bradford. *The Mariner's Dictionary*. New York: Weathervane Books, 1972.

Giffith, Bob. *Blue Water—A Guide to Self-Reliant Sailboat Cruising*. Boston: Sail Books, 1979.

Farrington, Tony. *Rescue in the Pacific*. Camden, ME: International Marine Publishing Co., 1996.

Henderson, Richard. *Sea Sense*. Camden, ME: International Marine Publishing Co., 1979.

Hinz, Earl R. *The Complete Book of Anchoring and Mooring*. Centreville, MD: Cornell Maritime Press, Inc., 1999.

Hiscock, Eric C. *Around the World in Wanderer III*. New York: Oxford University Press, 1956.

Hiscock, Eric C. *Cruising under Sail*. New York: Oxford University Press, 1981.

Jordan, Donald J. *Investigation of the Use of Drogues to Improve the Safety of Sailing Yachts and Life Rafts*. Report No. CG-D-37-84. Washington: US Coast Guard, 1984.

Lewis, David. *The Ship Would Not Travel Due West*. N.p.: Temple Press Books, 1961.

Manry, Robert. *Tinkerbelle*. New York: Harper & Row, 1966.

Mate, Ferenc. *The Finely Fitted Yacht* (2 vols.). New York: W.W. Norton, 1979; and Vancouver, B.C.: Albatross Publishing House, 1979.

Moitessier, Bernard. *Cape Horn: The Logical Route*. Bungay, Suffolk: Chaucer Press, 1969.

Mundle, Rob. *Fatal Storm*. Camden, ME: International Marine Publishing Co., 1999.

Norgrove, Ross. *The Cruising Life*. Camden, ME: International Marine Publishing Co., 1980.

Pardey, Lin and Larry. *Storm Tactics Handbook*. Arcata, CA: Paradise Cay Publications, 1995.

Pidgeon, Harry. *Around the World Singlehanded*. London: R. Hart-Davis, 1954.

Poynter, Daniel F. *The Parachute Manual*. North Quincy, MA: Self-published, 1972.

Robinson, William Albert. *To the Great Southern Sea*. London: Peter Davies Ltd., 1966.

Rousmaniere, John. *Fastnet, Force 10*. New York: W. W. Norton, 1980.

Shane, Victor. *Drag Device Data Base*. Summerland, CA: Para-Anchors International, 1998.

Shane, Victor. *Force 10 Imminent*. Edition One of the Newsletter. Summerland, CA: Para-Anchors International, August 1985.

Shane, Victor. *Standard Procedures of Parachute Sea-Anchoring*. Summerland, CA: Para-Anchors International, 1983.

Shewmon, Daniel. *Sea Anchors, Drogues and Salvage Bells*. Technical Report. Safety Harbor, FL: Shewmon, Inc., 1981.

Shewmon, Daniel. *The Sea Anchor & Drogue Handbook*. Safety Harbor, FL: Shewmon, Inc., 1998.

United States Yacht Racing Union. *Safety from Capsizing*. Final report in cooperation with the Society of Naval Architects and Marine Engineers. Newport, RI: USYRU, 1985.

Van Dorn, William G. *Oceanography and Seamanship*. New York: Dodd, Mead & Co., 1974.

Voss, John Claus. *The Venturesome Voyages of Captain Voss*. Sydney, B.C.: Gray's Publishing Ltd., 1949.

Walton-Smith, F.G. *The Seas in Motion*. New York: Thomas Y. Crowell Co., 1973.

Index

Series drogue: definition, 97, 112; characteristics, 112-115; rigging, (illustrated) 113; Jordan load advisory, 115; by Ace Sailmakers, 153; by Sailrite, 154

Shewmon, Daniel: mentioned, 40, 43-46, 49,107-109

Specialty sea anchor nomenclature note, 77

Storm oil: experiences, 133-134; quantity, 134, 136; dispersal, 133-138 *passim*; types, 135-136; temperature effect, 136; problems, 136-138 *passim*; dispersal container, (illustrated) 137

Sydney-Hobart Race (1998): wave height misinterpretation, 26-28; wave shapes, 32-33; Committee recommendations on drag devices, 140

Tilikum: early drag device user, 3-4

US Sailing: sea anchor size criteria, 39-40; multihull size guideline, 43

Voss, Capt. John: drag device pioneer, 3-5; mentioned, 89, 134

Warps, 91, 94-95, 134

Waves: properties, 18-19; forms, 19; swells, 19; related to Beaufort scale, 21-22; dimensions, 24, 26-29; time and fetch influence, (illustrated) 25; significant height, 26; spectrum, (illustrated) 27; rogue, 28; rhythm, 28-29; wind in opposition, 32-33

Waves - breaking: dynamics, 29, 31-32; shapes (illustrated) 30; multiple trains, 31-32

Waves - non-breaking: shapes, 20-21, (illustrated) 20, 21, 23; orbital surface motion, 21-24; surface motion (illustrated) 23

Wind drag coefficients: 143-144; boat examples, (illustrated) 145

About the Author

Earl Hinz has been sailing Pacific Ocean waters since 1958 accumulating 40,000 sea miles in racing and cruising sail boats. After retiring from the aerospace industry as an engineer in 1975 he took to cruising and writing as his second career ending up living aboard his boat between voyages in Honolulu for 15 years. He has owned a variety of boats including a 41-foot ketch and a 36-foot trawler.

Besides being an experienced sailor, Hinz is a published author and is widely known for his extensive magazine article writing. His hundreds of periodical contributions on Pacific cruising and contemporary boating can be found in such magazines as *Cruising World, SEA, Ocean Navigator, Multihulls, Latitudes & Attitudes, PassageMaker, Pacific, Glimpses of Micronesia and Pacifica*. As SEA's Technical Editor for five years, he conducted quantitative sea trials on 104 power and sailboats and sponsored dozens of technical tests on boat hardware and electronics.

Richard Rhodes, who drew the figures, is a noted marine illustrator retired from the staff of the University of Hawaii. Rhodes has designed a line of modern racing and charter catamarans as well as contemporary custom design Hawaiian racing and voyaging canoes. He is presently working on the archeological reconstruction drawings of several notable Marquesan monumental architecture sites.